Prophetic Spiritual Warfare t
by adding the power of pro
hidden in the unseen realm.
a certainty. More than just a
Warfare equips you with a w
authorities, the powers of this dark world, and spiritual forces of evil in the heavenly realms.

—Rabbi Eric Walker
Executive Director, Igniting a Nation Ministries

Prophetic Spiritual Warfare takes believers into heaven's war room by providing them with stealth spiritual tactics, strategies, and sound biblical revelation to use in this invisible battle against the archenemy of God—the devil. My friend apostolic leader Kathy DeGraw outlines throughout the pages of this book powerful, practical tools forged by God's Word for readers to win every unseen battle. She offers the equipping, inspiration, impartation, and revelation for you to form weapons that will prosper against the enemy before he can forge weapons that try to prosper against you. This book charges and encourages God's people to wage prophetic warfare over their prophetic destiny and with His supernatural assistance to victoriously fight the good fight on the invisible battlefield. This is a must-read work in these perilous times that I am so proud to recommend!

—Dr. Hakeem Collins
Founder, Champions International;
Author, *Unseen Warfare*, *Heaven Declares*,
and *Command Your Healing*

Apostle Kathy DeGraw has done it this time! This book is like having a treasure map given from heaven. It adds spiritual strategies and weapons to your arsenal that will pierce the kingdom of darkness when put into practice. As I read this book, I felt recharged, strengthened, and fearless—ready for combat! Exposing the darkness and revealing mysteries is something this woman of God does well. After you read this amazing book, you will become more aware of your surroundings and effective in your Christian walk. The one word I'd use to summarize this book: strategic!

—Apostle Luis Lopez, DD
Luis Lopez Media Ministries International;
Speaker; Author, *The Counterfeit Christian*

Kathy DeGraw has done an exceptional job explaining the unseen battle behind the prophetic in her latest book, *Prophetic Spiritual Warfare*. She intelligently reveals biblically that spiritual warfare must be prophetically led by the Holy Spirit in order to see supernatural breakthroughs, victories, deliverances, and healings. I highly endorse this powerful book of prophetic warfare strategies, tools, and spiritual weaponry for every believer, as a prophetic spiritual warrior, to learn how to engage and to conquer stealth attacks from our invisible adversaries.

—Naim Collins
Prophetic Voice;
Founder, Fan the Flames Global Ministries;
Author, *Realms of the Prophetic*

I've known Kathy for a few years, and during that time, I've known her as a frontline soldier for the kingdom of God. Not only has she wreaked havoc against the enemy on my behalf with her unwavering prayer covering; she has put a hurting on the kingdom of darkness with her writing, podcasts, meetings, and deliverance ministry. As she says in *Prophetic Spiritual Warfare*, "The devil will use our pasts, generational curses, and soul ties to gain a foothold in our lives," but we must "give no place to the devil." Kathy gives practical advice on how to take control of our thoughts, increase in spiritual discernment, and rebuke Satan. Read this book and learn from Kathy how to wage powerful, effective spiritual warfare every day with the Holy Spirit as your advocate.

—Shawn A. Akers
Online Managing Editor, Charisma Media

Do you want to get better and finally enter into your destiny? If so, *Prophetic Spiritual Warfare* is the book for you. Let's be frank, even when you have received the best teaching, warfare and attacks will happen. But when they do, with the help of this prophetic manual, the warfare will happen but *will not prosper*—and that's what you need to know. Your soul needs cleansing, and that is something this book will teach you to do all the time—and I mean daily. Finally, here is a book where wholeness and spiritual cleaning are going to lead you to the destiny you've only dreamed of. Get this book, and while you're at it, buy a copy for a friend!

—Steve Shultz
Founder, The Elijah List and Elijah Streams

In *Prophetic Spiritual Warfare*, Kathy DeGraw shares her deep heart desire to see people healed and delivered. She has experienced much over the years in spiritual warfare, and she has learned to overcome by releasing the prophetic and the love of Jesus. You will be encouraged by the revelatory truth that pours forth through her personal stories of victory, faith activations, and exercises in each chapter, which will help you develop the skills you need to learn to stand firm in your faith and defeat the enemy. You will also be blessed by her desire to see you draw intimately in relationship with the Lord. May God use this book to sharpen your tools for kingdom advancement.

—Dr. Candice Smithyman
Host, *Glory Road* and *Your Path to Destiny* on
It's Supernatural! Network

Kathy DeGraw is a deliverance minister whom God is using mightily in this generation. After reading these pages, I was challenged by the revelation knowledge the Lord has given this woman of God to write such a book. Her exposition on the various types of warfare and deliverance is excellent. It is pertinent for end-time Christians to be up to date with the move of the Holy Spirit. This book is relevant at a time like this, considering the problems many people are facing.

—Apostle/Prophet Bernard D. Evans
Overseer, Tabernacle Ruach Ha'Kodesh Christian Ministry;
Bernard D. Evans Ministries

Kathy DeGraw's *Prophetic Spiritual Warfare* is a spiritual warfare boot camp for sure! The authority, power, insight, revelation, and clear spiritual definition of this possibly complex topic is unlike what I have encountered in my personal study time. This book debunks the myths, fears, and prevalent lies tied to spiritual warfare. More interesting and unique is the prophetic part of this wonderful guide. Each chapter has an extensive and focused activation, prayer, and declaration guide. It ministers to the whole person as well as equips the body of Christ for the greater work of God.

—Beatriz Zaldana
Director, Convergence Ministry

Kathy DeGraw's latest literary work, *Prophetic Spiritual Warfare*, furnishes the reader with a bird's-eye view into the nefarious machinations of Satan's kingdom through the lens of prophetic ministry. In each chapter she equips the reader with spiritual warfare tools, such as proclamations, activations, prayers, and decrees, that they can use personally to overcome demonic influences that have infiltrated their lives. I highly recommend this engaging, interactive, transparent, and informative book, which will help you rid yourself of stubborn demons that desire to stop you from reaching your full potential in God.

—John Veal
CEO, John Veal Ministries;
Senior Pastor, Enduring Faith Christian Center

In this book Kathy asks, "Do you know the Holy Spirit? Can you call Him your friend?" If you want to know Him more or if you answered yes to her question, then this book will give you the principles and activations you need to know Him on a deeper level. Kathy is a seasoned apostolic warrior who will teach you how to hear God and prophesy, engage in spiritual warfare, activate your spiritual senses, and draw near to Jesus. *Prophetic Spiritual Warfare* is a word in season that will set a fire within you to run to the secret place.

—Jared Laskey
Cofounder, Fireborn Ministries;
Host, *Adventures in the Spirit With Jared Laskey* Podcast

Kathy DeGraw's book on prophetic spiritual warfare is a must-have in every believer's tool kit. It contains practical, easy-to-follow steps, strategies, and exercises that will thoroughly teach and equip readers to partner with the Holy Spirit to receive lasting breakthrough. Valuable for both new and seasoned Christians, Kathy's insights will help accelerate readers into the next level of their destiny.

—Joanna Adams
Author, *Closing the Door to Demons*;
Co-pastor, Eagles' Nest Fellowship

Apostle Kathy DeGraw has released a refreshing knowledge of the Holy Ghost as a teacher that most people are unaware of. Through *Prophetic Spiritual Warfare* you will be encouraged to trust the Holy Ghost to teach and guide you to lead others in deliverance as well as allow Him to lead you into deliverance for yourself. What a powerful revelation for so many people. With the Holy Ghost and Christ on your side, you can do all things (Phil. 4:13).

—Dr. Gina R. Prince
Christian Counselor;
Host, *Dr. Gina's Radio Chat*

This book is not just a book with information; it is a mighty arsenal of knowledge to equip and empower you and your family for the spiritual battles ahead. Warfare will come knocking on the door of our lives, but we can be prepared and ready to claim victory! Arm yourself with this book!

—Joel Yount
Cofounder, Spirit Fuel;
Host, *Spirit Fuel Live* Video Broadcast (www.spiritfuel.me)

PROPHETIC SPIRITUAL WARFARE

Kathy DeGraw

Most Charisma House Book Group products are available at special quantity discounts for bulk purchase for sales promotions, premiums, fund-raising, and educational needs. For details, call us at (407) 333-0600 or visit our website at www.charismahouse.com.

Prophetic Spiritual Warfare by Kathy DeGraw
Published by Charisma House
Charisma Media/Charisma House Book Group
600 Rinehart Road, Lake Mary, Florida 32746

Visit the author's website at www.kathydegrawministries.org.

Library of Congress Cataloging-in-Publication Data:
An application to register this book for cataloging has been submitted to the Library of Congress.

International Standard Book Number: 978-1-62999-971-5
E-book ISBN: 978-1-62999-972-2

21 22 23 24 25 — 987654321
Printed in the United States of America

To my husband, Ron DeGraw: your unfailing love and support put gratefulness in my heart and change countless lives. Thank you for naming my podcast show, Prophetic Spiritual Warfare, *which ultimately birthed this book. I appreciate your sacrifice of putting up with unseen warfare and constant deadlines. You allow me to travel the world, you research and figure out camera and recording equipment with no prior experience, and you obeyed the Lord in granting my request to get my puppy, Shiloh, when you didn't want a dog. You are a true man of God! I love you!*

TABLE OF CONTENTS

PREFACE

I CAN HONESTLY SAY that the Holy Spirit is my best friend. I ask, and He answers. I rely on Him to teach, guide, correct, and convict me. But it hasn't always been this way. My friendship with the Holy Spirit began after my husband, Ron, and I experienced a long, intense year of spiritual warfare several years ago. At the time, we were completely unfamiliar with spiritual warfare, and all we could do was rely on the Holy Spirit.

After that season of unprecedented spiritual attack, we relocated our family to our hometown in Michigan. I spent my time adjusting our kids to their new home and schools and focused on being a mom and wife. I didn't work outside the home, so I was able to spend the next two years prostrate on the carpet in the presence of the Father, getting to know Jesus and the Holy Spirit. I had one goal in mind: get to know the Trinity deeply.

During this time, I had many encounters and visions with Jesus. I would lie on the floor where it often felt like His face was in the carpet (many times I saw it there) as we dialogued back and forth. No deliverance minister cast out my demons or led me through the deliverance process. Jesus was my Deliverer. No one taught me about spiritual warfare. The Holy Spirit was my Teacher and Guide.

Life those years had been intense, but in the years that followed, I rested in the presence of the Lord and learned about healing and deliverance. I didn't seek to be prophetic or have a deliverance ministry; I simply desired to get to know Jesus intimately. I allowed the Holy Spirit to lead my prayer and worship time, breaking down strongholds and bringing me into the glory of God's presence. He directed which books I should study and taught me the Scriptures.

Those years of seeking the Holy Spirit birthed and launched me into deliverance ministry. I followed the Holy Spirit's leading in deliverance ministry for the next few years, and even though I didn't walk in prophetic ministry—often referred to as "the prophetic"—at that time, I had a keen sense of discernment and could see into the spiritual realm.

In 2009 the Holy Spirit convicted me of the prophetic call on my life. Up to that point, I never wanted anything to do with prophetic ministry because I had seen impure motives in people seeking it. Jesus had placed a prophetic mantle on me during an encounter I had with Him, which I will talk more about later. But I denied this call three times, and I had been running from it ever since. However, in 2009, I was finally obedient. I repented and embraced the prophetic call on my life—but at a limited level. I still wasn't fully using what the Lord had given me until I witnessed how it could empower me to conquer spiritual attacks through prayer and help me to see into a person's heart to break strongholds off his or her life. When I witnessed people being set free from demonic oppression in five minutes versus eight-hour sessions, I was all in! I'll share more about this in chapter 2.

I pray and allow Him to guide me through decisions, including where and when to travel, what to purchase, and what restaurant to eat at. I've relied on Him several times when discerning which regions He has called my team to travel to, minister to, and pray over. He's led us on prophetic ministry tours that we call Be Love Prophetic Tours. We've relied on

Him to know what city to go to, what route to take, and where to stop along the way for ministry, food, and lodging.

Along the way I started a podcast called *Prophetic Spiritual Warfare*, and I've given this book the same title. It's critical to know the meaning behind this title. Any book or podcast on spiritual warfare will explore combating spiritual obstacles and darkness, but *Prophetic Spiritual Warfare* emphasizes that the key to spiritual warfare is being led by the examples of Jesus in the Bible and the Holy Spirit's guidance. Being prophetically led by the Spirit of God means we partner with the Holy Spirit in everything we say and do and most importantly in our prayer time. The Spirit of God knows what needs to be prayed about and how it needs to be conquered. He knows each battle we face and how it relates to our past, present, and future. Therefore, when we partner with the Holy Spirit, He will lead us to victory. We can't do our spiritual walks alone; neither can we base them on a legalistic, man-made formula. We are spirit beings. Therefore, we must be led by the Holy Spirit.

Since prophetic spiritual warfare is conquering adversity while being prophetically led by the Holy Spirit, the core message of this book is surrendering yourself entirely to the Spirit of God. How do you allow the Spirit of the Lord to move through you uninhibited? If you want to be prophetic—and I'm sure you do because the title of this book grabbed your attention—then you need to learn how to move prophetically, which means to be continually led by the Spirit of God.

That's what makes this book different. It isn't just about spiritual warfare. It is about living a life sold out to the Holy Spirit. It teaches you how to partner with the Holy Spirit in prayer, personal devotion time, healing, deliverance, and all aspects of spiritual warfare. It is about becoming a prophetic generation of vessels the Holy Spirit can use—conduits of Him and His perpetual flow. Our lives are platforms given to the Holy Spirit to glorify the name of Jesus Christ and advance the kingdom of God.

Take this journey with me, and let's do life together. I learned from the Holy Spirit, and He is the best Teacher. I ask you not only to let Him be your Teacher and Guide through this book but also to allow Him to become your best friend. Use this book as a tool, as a starting point, and then spend time in the presence of the Holy Spirit and let Him instruct you further, as He did me.

It has always been my dream that people would be so desperate for healing, deliverance, or impartation that they would interrupt my preaching and run to the altar to receive whatever I was speaking about. The Holy Spirit led me to add that element of immediacy to this book. Therefore, I discuss a topic and give you tools to address it immediately. Prophetic exercises are implanted within the chapters, and each chapter closes with prophetic activations. You are not just learning about a subject; you are being activated.

To engage in prophetic spiritual warfare, you will need to pray intense warfare prayers to combat the powers of darkness. I provide in each chapter examples of faith proclamations and spiritual warfare declarations. And being a deliverance minister, I've loaded this book with deliverance prayers and information about additional resources where you can receive freedom or learn how to minister freedom to others.

All these tools are provided to equip and activate you in the prophetic, which is the most effective kind of spiritual warfare. I encourage you to purchase a journal or notebook to record what I believe God wants to speak to you during these activation sections. Keep it nearby as you read this book, and write in it often. What you hold in your hands is not merely a book of knowledge. This is a book of revelation, impartation, and activation.

The devil has stolen your destiny long enough. The battles that have been waged against you must cease. It's time to learn how to conquer battles and manifest your destiny as you follow the Holy Spirit's leading! Don't wait another minute. Turn the page and get started.

OPENING PROPHETIC WORD

I FEEL THE PROPHETIC *realm stirring. I feel a revival well coming forth. I see in the spirit a swirling of the Spirit around you, the reader. I see the Ruach Ha'Kodesh, the breath of God, encompassing you and surrounding you. The Lord says, "This is a new season—a season of revelation, a season of oneness with the Holy Spirit. The Lord says you are going to get to know the Holy Spirit on a new level. Revelation, increase, and release are coming your way. Old things are gone; old ways of operating in the flesh and the natural are going to pass." He says, "You are going to lean on and rely upon My Spirit. I sent My Son Jesus to die for you so He could leave you a helper. The Spirit has been here since before time. I have released Him to be your helper. Now let Him be your helper. Allow Him to be everything you need. You don't have to do this in your own strength. The Spirit is battle ready and knows what it takes to conquer warfare in your life. Partner with Him. Depend on Him. Don't take a step without Him. He will get you through the battle quickly and with ease. You have fought in your own strength, and you are tired and weary. With the Spirit on your side engaging in the battle prophetically for you, there will be no more tiredness. You will enjoy partnering with the Holy Spirit and what He can do for you and through you. Your life is a platform for the Holy Spirit; reach out and invite Him in to release His Spirit out of you. You are on a one-way track, a path that leads to the Holy Spirit. Stay on the path. Receive everything you can from Him so you are battle ready with the greatest team of three on your side, the Father, Jesus the Son, and the Holy Spirit."*

Chapter 1

WHAT IS SPIRITUAL WARFARE?

IF YOU ARE new to the concept of spiritual warfare, you are not alone. I knew nothing about spiritual warfare when my family found itself at the epicenter of the most intense spiritual battle we've ever faced. But the Holy Spirit taught me everything I needed to know, and in this book I aim to draw from that experience and help you discover Him as your Teacher and Guide in the same way.

Many years ago, when my husband, Ron, and I were green in ministry and pastoring our first church, we were thrown into the worst spiritual battle of our lives. We had no idea about what we were up against or how to fight it. We didn't know about our authority in Christ or the power of our words. All we knew was that we were in an all-out war, and our church, community, and family were being attacked. We also knew God had us on a mission. We were going to stand strong in the Lord no matter what was thrown at us. The battle was intense, but we didn't give up.

The Bible says, "No weapon that is formed against you shall prosper" (Isa. 54:17). It does not say a weapon won't *come*, but that it won't *prosper*. In our family's case a spiritual attack of sickness and death came to visit our family over a period of two years, but it did not prevail. Extreme stress and fatigue from pushing so hard in ministry landed me in bed for six weeks, unable to lift my head. I was diagnosed with high blood pressure, a condition I was healed of years later after a time of prayer and fasting. Later that year, our son, Dillon, who was ten, was attacked with four different sicknesses, and we were told we had to get him to the hospital within four hours before his organs would begin shutting down. I was so oblivious to spiritual warfare and authority that I thought God was *causing* the sickness in our son so people would pray and be led back on the road to Christ.

I now know the spirit of death was attacking our family. It continued to assault my husband, Ron, a year later. He started feeling very ill, and we went to the hospital. He had elevated white blood cell counts. I stood by his hospital bed, not praying for healing but praying, "God, if taking him to heaven would bring glory to Your name and release the pain, do it." They could not diagnose my husband and sent him home. His appendix burst overnight. The next morning they called and said the X-rays were read wrong and I needed to get him back there for emergency surgery. The thing that saved his life when his appendix burst was that the poison stayed in one part of his stomach instead of traveling throughout his body. He was in the hospital for a week and then sent home to further recover.

Paranormal activity and demonic visitation began to happen in our home. There would be no radios on, and yet we would hear music through the air ducts. Our son, Dillon, had two visitations from the enemy, where the enemy said, "I am going to kill you." Our daughter Lauren, at four years of age, had demons with glowing red eyes visit her nightly. These and other manifestations continued until we consulted with a Spirit-filled pastor friend of ours who happened to know about spiritual warfare. She taught us the basics of spiritual housecleaning, where you go through your home to discern the spiritual atmosphere and then pray to expel any demonic activity and call forth blessings and peace. When we anointed Lauren's bed and room with oil and began to speak out prayer declarations against the attacks, they stopped completely.

Then spiritual assault took on a new form with word curses and people within the church conjuring up and admitting to spreading lies about us. They had no shame as they revealed their plans of destruction against us, and they would coerce people into joining them in their plan to run us out of the community and church. They desired control and could control everything in the community except us. The control was being triggered by the witchcraft activity in that region. When witchcraft principalities are in a region, they can attack and lure people into wreaking havoc, even if they don't know what they are doing is witchcraft.

These people were angry and hurting because of their pasts, and control was a way to deal with their pain. In the beginning they were subconsciously participating in witchcraft by not knowing their actions were part of spiritual warfare tactics the enemy deploys. However, later on, one of the people involved in this group admitted to us they hired a medium and began practicing witchcraft through cursing, séances, palm reading, and other witchcraft activities.

We knew we weren't fighting people. We were fighting the principalities operating through them. (See Ephesians 6:12.) We must separate the principality from the person, which I'll discuss in depth in another chapter.

If that wasn't spiritual boot camp, I don't know what is. We were thrown into an all-out battle with no experience. A person with over thirty years' ministry experience mediated the situation, and she told us that most leaders would have quit ministry after what we experienced, but not us. With the Holy Spirit's help, it made us stronger.

I believe God often gives us our hardest assignment first to make everything else look easy. Being a deliverance minister, I know there are different levels of deliverance and a variety of demonic experiences. When I minister to a person who has been hammered by the enemy, I tell the person, "God will use you mightily!" The prophetic side of me gets excited because I know the victory awaiting the person on the other side. If that person could endure what he or she did, I know he or she will be able to get through anything.

When we finally left the region, we stopped the vehicle, got out, and wiped off our feet in accordance with Matthew 10:14. We didn't know about spiritual authority and demonic operations, but we did know enough to do a prophetic act and wipe off our feet as the Bible states. The Lord was with us in so many ways. It was a difficult experience, but I wouldn't be here today writing this book or functioning as a prophetic deliverance minister without it.

SPIRITUAL WARFARE DEFINED

We are in an unseen, invisible war between good and evil, darkness and light. Spiritual warfare is when Satan and his kingdom of darkness, lies, and destruction come against God and His kingdom of light, love, and goodness. Friction and conflict happen in the spiritual realm, and Satan comes to oppose God's prophecies and will for your life.

There is a direct correlation between the natural and the spiritual. What happens in the spiritual occurs in the natural and vice versa. A collision is happening in the spiritual realm at all times—and you are already involved in it whether you like it or not. Ignorance is not bliss, and being unaware of the war does not minimize its effects. Satan relentlessly instigates attacks to wear out those who seek God and desire to advance His kingdom. He will attempt to wreak havoc in your life any way he can. An unseen war not embraced by believers is a strategic way he can attack on the sly.

I shared my family's experiences with you for two reasons. First, I wanted you to understand where I'm coming from and how I learned the insights I'm sharing with you in this book. Second, I wanted to give you a picture of what spiritual warfare can look like. Our battle was real, and even though we could see people and realized the attacks were demonic, we were fighting an invisible war. We couldn't see the dark forces behind the medical ailments, emotional trauma, and witchcraft spirits. This is the essence of spiritual warfare. Whether or not you experience overt attacks as we did, it is important to know that you are taking part in an unseen war. It's not something you choose; everyone is born into it. Everything you say and do affects it, giving power to one side or the other. That's why it's so important to be led by the Holy Spirit.

It's also important to know who you're up against.

The Adversary

Who is our adversary? The devil was once one of God's angels. His name was Lucifer. He was the angel in charge of worship in heaven. Lucifer rebelled against God, and as a result God cast him down to earth. Here's what the Bible says about it.

> How you are fallen from heaven, O Lucifer, son of the morning! How you are cut down to the ground, you

> who weaken the nations! For you have said in your heart, "I will ascend into heaven, I will exalt my throne above the stars of God; I will sit also on the mount of the congregation, in the recesses of the north; I will ascend above the heights of the clouds, I will be like the Most High." Yet you shall be brought down to Hell, to the sides of the pit.
>
> —Isaiah 14:12–15

> He said to them, "I saw Satan as lightning fall from heaven."
>
> —Luke 10:18

> The great dragon was cast out, that ancient serpent called the Devil and Satan, who deceives the whole world. He was cast down to the earth, and his angels were cast down with him.
>
> —Revelation 12:9

Now that we've covered how he became our adversary, let's take a look at three things the Bible tells us about the devil.

1. He is a thief.

The devil is a thief who comes to steal, kill, and destroy anything and everything in your life. "The thief does not come except to steal, and to kill, and to destroy. I have come that they may have life and that they may have it more abundantly" (John 10:10, NKJV). Stealing, killing, and destroying are spiritual warfare. The devil tries to make sure we don't have the abundant life that Jesus said we could have.

Jesus wants us to have abundant life. Attacks that lead to a negative result are never the result of the Lord sending something forth to hinder or punish us. God does not make people sick to use them or teach them lessons. He is a Father who wants the best for His children. It is the enemy who comes to steal, kill, and destroy, while the Lord's intention is for us to have abundant life.

2. He is wicked.

"We know that we are of God, and the whole world lies under the sway of the wicked one" (1 John 5:19, NKJV). When Satan was cast down to earth, he was given authority over the earth. We live under the sway of the wicked one until we come to know Jesus and His glorious power! Unfortunately the enemy has far too much influence on the earth, which is why we see sin, crime, unforgiveness, addiction, and bondage. However, Jesus came to the earth to make right what was wrong. He gave us His authority.

3. He is a liar.

"You are of your father the devil, and you want to do the desires of your father. He was a murderer from the beginning, and does not stand in the truth, because there is no truth in him. When he lies, he speaks from his own nature, for he is a liar and the father of lies" (John 8:44). The devil is the father of lies, and he will lie to us. His lies can appear as thoughts we take hold of, things someone said to us or about us, or manipulation. The devil will use our pasts, generational curses, and soul ties to gain a foothold in our lives. I'll discuss these more later.

When we haven't been taught about spiritual warfare and how cunning the enemy is, we will take in the lies and begin to believe them. After a while these lies we take in become strongholds in our lives, and when we don't change our thoughts and behavior patterns, the strongholds can become strongmen, which are demonic spirits. To ensure strongmen do not enter and occupy our souls, we must quickly capture all the enemy's lies and give no place to the devil. Capturing the lie means recognizing the lie. When a thought comes into your mind, test it by discerning if it lines up with the Word of God. Is it something that would have a result that agrees with Scripture? If not, dismiss it instead of entertaining it.

Give no place to the devil by taking control of your thoughts so the lie does not torment you and cause you anxiety, anger, or fear. As we take unproductive and negative thoughts in and they stay captured in our minds, we entertain them instead of dismissing the thoughts. When we know Scripture, we can conquer our thoughts with the Word and replace a negative that might cause us to feel defeated or fearful with a positive, a truth of God's Word and what He says about our situations.

Prophetic Exercise: No Place for the Devil

List 1–3 things that occupy your thoughts. What consumes you in a negative way? Where haven't you been able to receive breakthrough? What brings forth stress, depression, or fear?

Next, think about what Scripture says regarding those unproductive thoughts. For example, if the thought is that you will never have enough, test it against the Scriptures, which say God is your provider (Phil. 4:19). Therefore, remove the lie now and lean on Scripture. Practice taking every thought captive. If it does not align with Scripture, dismiss it.

Ask the Holy Spirit to convict you when you begin to have unproductive thinking and when the enemy is tormenting you. Ask the Holy Spirit to partner with you to conquer your thoughts by convicting and correcting you. Rely on Him to be your friend and lead you through spiritual growth in this area.

We have the final victory. No matter how hard the devil tries to defeat us, his fate is written in the Word of God, and he loses! He is defeated! Rest assured that whatever you go through, whatever you try to help someone through, it can be conquered. God's Word says that we are conquerors. "Yet in all these things we are more than conquerors through Him who loved us" (Rom. 8:37, NKJV). We are conquerors, and the devil is defeated!

Now that we understand our adversary, let's examine the spiritual forces at work.

Angels vs. Demons

For many people, it is easier to believe in an angel than a demon. People choose to believe in things that make them happy and help them. Hebrews 1:14 tells us that angels are sent as ministers. They are here to help guide us and protect us, among many other functions that angels perform. Most people would rather talk about the help angels give us than about how demons can attack us or their role on earth.

Many Christians don't even believe in demons. I can't count the number of people who have come to my ministry for a deliverance session because a friend told them it was the greatest experience. This is a caution for me. It tells me they don't know what they are getting themselves into. When this happens, I start by asking whether they believe in angels. The usual reply is yes. Then I ask if they believe in demons. Most people either hesitate or say no.

The truth is we live in a fallen world. Satan was once the

beautiful angel Lucifer, but he allowed pride and rebellion to arise. In the Scriptures we read that one-third of the angels were cast out of heaven with him. How can we read the Bible and think demons don't exist? We can't pick and choose which parts of the Bible to believe and which to ignore. The fight between good and evil is a very real battle, and Satan opposes anything that is God's will, including God's plan for your life.

THE BATTLE PLAN

To defeat the enemy, we must know his plans and purposes, expose them, and eradicate his attacks. How do we fight and resist something we can't see? Knowledge is power, and when we follow the example of Jesus and prophetic insights from the Holy Spirit, we will have everything we need to know to engage and win the battle set before us.

The forces of darkness have one main assignment: creating obstacles and roadblocks to delay and detour our destinies. We want to move up in our spiritual walks and forward in our destinies. Demonic spirits attempt to establish barriers and set up perimeters to prevent our forward movement.

The devil causes these restrictions in our lives, but Jesus came to teach us how to fight strategically. When we follow the ministry of deliverance Jesus exuded—how He prayed, cast out demons, healed the sick, and ministered—we will learn how to defeat the devil. Jesus conquered the powers of death and destruction at the cross. He defeated the enemy by His notable victory. We need to be an extension of that victory, walking in the fullness of God and manifesting His kingdom on earth.

This cannot be done with natural tools but rather by

relying on the strength of the Holy Spirit. Natural wars with military artillery are fought with tanks, missiles, and guns. However, it is the strategies of those in command that set up how to attack the enemy. Even though there are natural battle tools, you need to know how to move strategically, which is done with study, experience, and brainstorming with other military commanders.

In the spiritual realm we, too, need insights on how to move strategically. We can move in the natural, fighting with Scripture, praying on our knees, and reading books on spiritual combat, but some of these can be made up of formulated strategies. Moving in the Spirit is just that: moving in the Spirit and following Him as our weaponry commander. Allow Him to show you how to move strategically. Get to know the Holy Spirit and yield to Him. This empowers you to fight and win an invisible war.

As a natural military commander tells which gun to fire first and how much ammunition to put forth at the enemy, it is the same with the Holy Spirit. He can tell us when and what scripture to release. He can lead us to pray in tongues or decree and declare in our native language. He gives us strategic moves to come against the enemy if we follow His direction instead of the knowledge we have gained in the natural. It is my deepest desire that as you read this book, you become equipped to allow the Holy Spirit to lead in everything you do and to conquer military battles in the spiritual realm.

It's Time for Activation

Each chapter in this book concludes with It's Time for Activation. I will lead you through steps that empower and equip you for prophetic spiritual warfare. Take this journey with me through the prayers of repentance, renunciation, breaking agreement, impartation, and activation. (Please note: I take a deep dive on the concept of breaking agreement in chapter 13.) Learn to pray and speak audibly into the spiritual realm with faith and warfare declarations. Further equip yourself for prophetic spiritual warfare through the spiritual activation assignments. Get ready to be equipped for spiritual warfare that is prophetically led by the Holy Spirit!

Prayer of Repentance, Renunciation, and Breaking Agreement

Jesus, forgive me for any legalism and unbelief I have had about spiritual warfare. I thank You for knowledge, and I repent if, at any time, I did not take Your Word or spiritual warfare seriously. I break agreement with any demonic infiltration of my soul. I call off all demonic attacks. Help me to understand the Scriptures and what You would want me to learn. I thank You that I have the Holy Spirit to partner with me as I learn about the spiritual realm. I break agreement with any false teaching that was received in my heart and mind. In Jesus' name, amen.

Impartation and Activation Prayer

Holy Spirit, I receive You as my teacher and instructor. Come and convict me of truth versus lies and light versus darkness. Help me walk in the light and love of God. Holy Spirit, eradicate anything dark out of me so I can live on fire for the Lord with the fullness of God manifesting in all areas of my life.

I thank Jesus for leaving me with the greatest helper. Holy Spirit, I receive Your help. Ignite me to be a frontline battle worker for Your kingdom. Assist me in continuing to defeat the devil in my life and the lives of others. Turn me into a prayer warrior and a powerful weapon against the enemy's camp. I love You, Holy Spirit, and I trust You for my future. In Jesus' name, amen.

Prophetic Proclamations (Faith Declarations)

Prophesy over yourself by praying audibly these prophetic faith declarations. Pray with ownership and expectation to see the manifestation:

I ask You, God, to order, direct, and assign angels to go forth and assist me in defeating spiritual attacks.

I announce to the demonic kingdom that I am armed, dangerous, and battle ready. I am empowered on high with the Holy Spirit.

I declare I am a warrior for Christ. The power of the Holy Spirit will annihilate the battle set before me.

I speak and declare I have an artillery full of scriptures to combat every evil force. The Holy Spirit is on my side, and nothing shall be impossible for me.

I will fulfill my marching orders to advance the

kingdom of God. I walk in my prophetic destiny in Jesus' name.

Spiritual Activation

Activation can come in the natural or supernatural. When we practice what we learn, we can increase the acceleration of what we received. Our faith grows as we implement what we learned. Activate what you learned by practicing these three spiritual warfare exercises.

1. Study angels and their involvement in the earth. Through a time of prayer ask God to release His angels to assist you in times of need.
2. Remember God's faithfulness. What spiritual warfare have you experienced? How have you witnessed the Lord's intervention in your situation to help you through the warfare? Look back and discover where He was faithful. It will help you trust Him in your present situation.
3. Study the adversary. There are several names and characteristics of the evil one, Satan, in the Bible. Study his names and their definitions to expose how he operates. This will help you to be on the offense instead of the defense when attacks arise.

Spiritual Warfare Declarations

Pray on the offense, not the defense. Protect yourself in the natural and spiritual by speaking out warfare prayers and declarations to bind and restrict every evil force against you. Speak these prayers audibly to bind and restrict demonic attacks.

> I dismiss any and every thought contrary to the Word of God. I speak and declare that I take every thought captive, exude my authority, and dismiss evil powers that would penetrate my mind.
>
> I bind and restrict the enemy from attacking my knowledge and comprehension as I go forward in this book to learn about prophetic spiritual warfare.
>
> I destroy every demonic attack sent against me to block and paralyze me from moving forward in the things of the Spirit.
>
> I demolish and forcefully tear down every demonic tower erected on my behalf. I order and direct every demonic commander to cease its activities against me.
>
> In Jesus' name I remove my birthdate and birthright from every demonic target written with my name on it.

Chapter 2

WALK IN THE PROPHETIC

I RAN FROM THE prophetic call on my life for five years. Spiritually speaking, I had my track shoes on, and I ran as hard and fast as I could. I didn't want any part of it because I had seen prophetic ministry abused and used as a type of "Christian witchcraft." Prophets would come into town, and people would flock to their conferences to get a word. Meanwhile, other Spirit-led events would lag in attendance because they weren't prophesying over everybody.

The lack of purity was a big turnoff for me. People would rather run to a person operating in the prophetic gift or office than to the Holy Spirit directly for a word. I took 2 Peter 1:21 seriously: "For prophecy never came by the will of man, but holy men of God spoke as they were moved by the Holy Spirit" (NKJV). I found it hard to believe that prophets were always being moved by the Spirit when people put such a high demand on them to give prophetic words.

I didn't even realize I had a prophetic call on my life until one day several years ago when Ron and I were attending a pastoral conference. As we sat in a session taught by Benny Hinn, the Lord suddenly appeared to me in a vision. I closed my eyes, and I saw the Lord. I was unaware of my surroundings because the vision was so intense. I couldn't tell you what Pastor Benny was saying except that he began talking about the prophetic.

I still remember the vision vividly. Jesus appeared to me and said He had a prophetic mantle for me. So many emotions raged through me. I didn't feel worthy. I didn't understand why He was calling me, and then He said, "I've called you to bring balance back to the prophetic." Like Peter, I denied Him three times. (See John 18.) He said I had to take the mantle.

I ran and ran from this calling until I finally submitted to it in 2009. I started to operate in the prophetic, but even then I was content with what would bubble up and never tried to stir up the gift. I didn't know all the different facets of the prophetic at that time. I was content to release a beginner's level of prophecy of edification, exhortation, and comfort. I believe a part of me still needed healing from the distorted and coveted prophetic gifts I had observed.

The Holy Spirit stretched me out of my comfort zone, giving me different instructions to increase my prophetic abilities. The Lord is a gentleman, leading and guiding you through your self-perceived insufficiencies. One day He used prophetic insight and my seer ability to help me set someone free from demonic bondage. Witnessing how a prophetic anointing could see into the heart of a person and set him free in five minutes instead of eight hours was all it took. I repented, cried out my disobedience, and embraced the prophetic call on my life.

You have a call too. I am sure some of you right now are running from it. I know you are, because, as I am writing this, the Holy Spirit is telling me prophetically right now that you are. I'm sure you've heard sayings such as "You can run, but you can't hide," or "You can't outrun God." You know as well as I do that God will catch up with you, and sooner or later you will end up submitting, so you might as well make it sooner and save yourself the trouble. Trust me—I've had to cut up my shoes as a prophetic act of submission to signify that I was done running from God.

EMBRACE YOUR DESTINY

Jonah tried to run from God. The Lord desired Jonah to be His prophetic voice, "But Jonah got up to flee to Tarshish from the presence of the LORD" (Jon. 1:3). The Lord wanted Jonah's attention, so He created a storm on the sea and put the ship in danger. The sailors were afraid of the storm and cast lots and inquired of Jonah why this was happening (vv. 4–8).

They were concerned for their lives, so Jonah instructed them to throw him into the sea (v. 12). "Now the LORD appointed a great fish to swallow Jonah. And Jonah was in the belly of the fish three days and three nights" (v. 17). The Lord got Jonah's attention with the storm, but the Lord still needed Jonah's obedience. While in the fish's belly, Jonah finally submitted to God's call. (See Jonah 2.)

God caught up with Jonah. Jonah could run, but he couldn't hide. You can run, but you can't hide. The Lord told me when I was running, "Kathy, every day that you don't prophesy, someone misses out on being blessed by the word I have to give them." Ouch, Lord! I'm sure you may have some ouches you need to address, as Jonah and I did.

Prophetic Exercise: Conviction

Let's stop and reflect. Would you allow the Holy Spirit to convict your heart? In what areas of your life have you been running and hiding from God? Have you been disobedient and lacked discipline regarding the Lord's directions? Is there something He told you to do or give up that you haven't yet? In a journal or notebook write about the conviction you may be receiving. Ask the Holy Spirit to give you a battle plan for how to change and become obedient to the call of God on your life.

Allow the Holy Spirit to lead you to a plan of action. It's time to take off your running shoes. The Bible says, "For many are called, but few are chosen" (Matt. 22:14). Be the one who is called *and* chosen. Don't be called and not fulfill your assignment.

Elijah had his greatest victory and felt defeated on the same day. God had to anoint Elisha in his place. Don't make God send someone else to accomplish what He has set for you. Complete your assignment and persevere with all diligence. "Let us run with endurance the race that is set before us" (Heb. 12:1).

If you want to walk and move in the prophetic, you need to allow the Holy Spirit to arise from within you and come out of you. Jesus said, "The kingdom of God is within you" (Luke 17:21). It is in you, and the Spirit wants to manifest it out of you. His kingdom isn't in you solely for your benefit; it is in you so you can share it with others.

Accept the call of God and the way He wants you to minister. If He called you to it, He will lead you through it. Cast down your flesh so you can walk in His Spirit. "Walk in the Spirit, and you shall not fulfill the lust of the flesh. For the flesh lusts against the Spirit, and the Spirit against the flesh. These are in opposition to one another, so that you may not do the things that you please" (Gal. 5:16–17). Live a life surrendered to the Spirit. Give up your flesh and your agenda for His will to be manifested on the earth through your life. Remember, being prophetically led by the Spirit of God means we partner with the Holy Spirit. We allow and receive

His conviction and instructions. Build a deep relationship with the Holy Spirit, and learn to yield to Him. Develop an intimate relationship with Him, and learn to hear His voice and obey His directions.

SURRENDER YOUR SOUL

Surrender your soul and yield to the Spirit. Give up your flesh and all entitlements to your life and destiny. Submit yourself unconditionally to the Lord. Give up your wants and desires for His. Accomplish His will, advance His kingdom, and release His love. It should be first and foremost in your life. Jesus crucified His flesh so that we may have life. When we crucify our flesh, we truly begin to live. "I have been crucified with Christ. It is no longer I who live, but Christ who lives in me. And the life I now live in the flesh, I live by faith in the Son of God, who loved me and gave Himself for me" (Gal. 2:20). Receive this scripture, and change your thoughts to believe that it is no longer you who lives, but "Christ in you, the hope of glory" (Col. 1:27).

Many times over my years in ministry, I remember having to give up my wants, dreams, and desires for what God's will was for my life. Often I'd go kicking and screaming, "God, why isn't this happening? Why isn't this door open? Why didn't You call me to do this instead of that?" Can you relate? If I'm honest, I still kick and scream a little from time to time.

The problem with our flesh and agenda is that if the Lord showed us our full destinies, we'd take the ball and run with it, instead of allowing Him to guide us and mature us as we wait for His timing. We must submit our will to His. My saying is "My life is not my own; it belongs to the One on the throne."

You may have to cast down your flesh several times. It might not work the first time you try, and you may pick up control again. When that happens, dust yourself off, repent of your failures and the times you wanted to do things in your strength, and yield to the One who sits on the throne.

Besides, most of the time, He gives you the desires of your heart because they are His desires that He gave to you. "Delight yourself in the LORD, and He will give you the desires of your heart" (Ps. 37:4). "Seek first the kingdom of God and His righteousness, and all these things shall be given to you" (Matt. 6:33).

I used to put God on a spiritual wrestling mat whenever He called me to move in a direction I wasn't thrilled about. It would be as if I were trying to slam dunk the Holy Spirit on that wrestling mat. Like Jacob, I've learned it's easier not to wrestle with God. He always wins! When we submit our flesh and do what He has called us to do, we win too!

Do whatever you have to do to surrender. Fast, pray, and worship! Lay yourself on the altar the way Abraham put Isaac on the altar. I love the story of faith, perseverance, and love that Abraham had for the Lord when confronted with laying his son Isaac on the altar to be slain. (See Genesis 22.) I think about the days he had to spend preparing. He had to cut the wood, pack their bags and food, and make the long journey. It is a story of such obedience, discipline, commitment, dedication, and everything else our Father wants to see from a faithful servant.

Prophetic Exercise: Surrender

Are you ready to completely surrender as Abraham did? Have you been convicted so far? Don't wait another second. Speak out and decree this prayer.

God, You can have all of me! I surrender to You! I exchange my agenda for Yours! Let Your will be done in my life. In Jesus' name I bind and restrict my flesh from activating. I proclaim I am submissive. I go forth with an eager expectancy of what You will do in my life. I repent of all disobedience to Your will. I trust You! I will walk with You and not against You. I submit to You! I love You, Lord, and I give You my life completely and with no reservations. In Jesus' name, amen.

Often we need to do a prophetic action, something in the natural to correlate to the spiritual breakthrough. Consider writing your surrender on a piece of paper and burning the paper or writing it on a sticky note and putting it on a cross you have in your home.

Begin a time of consecration and dedication unto the Lord, such as a time of prayer, fasting, or solitude. Spend time and seek the Holy Spirit. Ask Him to root out every part of you that does not align with the Word of God. It may be uncomfortable and unfamiliar; however, as you allow the Holy Spirit to remove soul wounds, negative behavior patterns, and demonic strongholds, you will feel victorious and empowered! The experience of brokenness is never pleasant, but the results are fruitful and productive for the kingdom of God!

Receive Power

The Holy Spirit empowers us to operate in the prophetic and to have the full manifestation of the Spirit inside us. We must get everything out of us that is not of the Lord. We must become less, and He must become more. A key reason for this is that we cannot hear effectively from the Holy Spirit if our flesh is in the way. We can hear three sources from within the spiritual realm: the enemy, ourselves, and the Spirit of God. Operating prophetically depends on hearing the voice of the Lord clearly, accurately, and unquestioningly. A deep relationship with the Holy Spirit is pertinent to know His voice and be close enough to Him that we desire to act on the instructions He imparts to us.

Our God exists in three persons, and one person of the Godhead is the Holy Spirit. A relationship with each person of the Trinity is vital in our spiritual walks. Get to know the Holy Spirit and His characteristics. He is the Spirit of revelation. (See Ephesians 1:17.) Walking in close communion with Him will increase your prophetic ability.

Do you know the Holy Spirit? Can you call Him your friend? The only way to answer yes to these questions is to develop a relationship with the Holy Spirit by spending time in the presence of the Lord. When you do, you will discover that the Holy Spirit is a friend, counselor, and the Spirit of wisdom and fire. He teaches, instructs, and listens. He assists in interpreting and applying the Scriptures. Jesus left us with a helper; He is the Holy Spirit. He is my best friend, and I hope He becomes yours too!

Receive the Holy Spirit

Ministering through prophetic gifts is contingent on receiving the Holy Spirit in His fullness. The prophetic has many levels and operations. They all are interconnected and have one common source: they flow out of the baptism of the Holy Spirit. It all began in the Upper Room on the day of Pentecost.

> When the day of Pentecost had come, they were all together in one place. Suddenly a sound like a mighty

> rushing wind came from heaven, and it filled the whole house where they were sitting. There appeared to them tongues as of fire, being distributed and resting on each of them, and they were all filled with the Holy Spirit and began to speak in other tongues, as the Spirit enabled them to speak.
>
> —Acts 2:1–4

The scripture says that "they were all filled with the Holy Spirit." The baptism of the Holy Spirit enables the gifts of the Spirit to be released through us. I like to use the analogy of mowing your lawn on a humid ninety-degree day. You are hot and sweaty. Would you rather have half a glass of water or a full glass that overflows with water? Our spiritual lives can be compared with a hot day. Do you only want a portion of the Holy Spirit, as in that half glass of water? Or do you want to be filled to overflowing with the Holy Spirit?

Jesus came so we could be filled and baptized with the Holy Spirit and fire (Matt. 3:11). When we overflow with the Holy Spirit, we can operate in the gifts of the Spirit as listed in 1 Corinthians 12. Specifically the gifts of wisdom, knowledge, faith, tongues, discerning of spirits, and prophecy will help you move and operate in the prophetic.

Audible Prayer to Receive the Baptism of the Holy Spirit

> *Lord, You said, "If I ask." I ask now for the Spirit of the Lord, the Holy Spirit, to come on me in power and might. Jesus, baptize me in Your Spirit and fire! I receive the baptism of the Holy Spirit with fire and evidence. Holy Spirit, I want and desire more of You and Your gifts. Baptize me with*

the power to operate in and release Your gifts. I receive the empowerment and infilling of the Holy Spirit so I am overflowing. Touch me now! Holy Spirit, release Your fire upon me. Baptize me in the fire and power of the Holy Spirit. Fire of God, come upon me now. I believe and I receive in Jesus' name. Amen!

Operate in the Prophetic

Being led prophetically by God's Spirit is a trust factor; it builds our relationship with the Lord as we trust the Spirit of God to move through us. Doubt and unbelief must be evacuated from our lives. God can and does still speak to His people today, and even though that may not always be audible, you can connect your spirit man to the Holy Spirit.

Releasing the prophetic is a phrase that means to release words based on the gift of prophecy or office of prophet. (See 1 Corinthians 12:8–11 and Ephesians 4:11.) Moving in the prophetic is an extension of the Holy Spirit and takes us beyond what we know. Different functions of the prophetic are releasing a word, prophetically preaching (being led by the Spirit rather than notes), and ministering prophetically with seer insights to release a word over someone or lead that person to experience healing and deliverance.

These prophetic functions highly depend on how much we trust the Holy Spirit as we receive revelation. The revelation then needs to be turned into impartation, activation, and application. Prophetic spiritual warfare is how to operate prophetically through the Holy Spirit to engage in spiritual warfare. The revelation imparted by the Holy Spirit conquers powers of darkness effectively.

Manifest Your Prophecies

Prophetic words spoken over our lives are road maps to our destiny. They are divine inspiration from the Spirit of God to lead us in a forward direction to release the kingdom of God. The Holy Spirit uses people to release prophetic words over our lives. Additionally we can receive prophetic insights directly from the Holy Spirit. Paul tells us that "we prophesy in part" (1 Cor. 13:9). Once the prophetic word is received, you need to do your part. Your part is to bring the prophecy forth to manifestation.

Prophetic Exercise:
Call Forth Your Prophetic Words

1. Test the word, and seek the Holy Spirit for accuracy (1 John 4:1).
2. Check the word, and see whether it aligns with Scripture (1 Thess. 5:21).
3. Write a prayer declaration based on the word you received. (See my book *SPEAK OUT*.)
4. Proclaim audibly for the word to manifest (Job 22:28).

In addition to the steps above, I have created a free e-course that I believe will give you helpful information on manifesting your prophetic words. (See the appendix.)

Years ago the majority of prophetic words I had thus far received had manifested because I continually made a demand on them. I prayed, declared, and took my authority to see the fulfillment of those words. I then inquired of the Lord to release more prophetic words over my life because I had experienced the results of most of mine. People become unsettled while they wait for their prophetic words to manifest, but when we understand we have to co-labor with the Spirit of God through prayer, we will see our words manifest.

Trust is the most crucial element to walk in the prophetic. When I began to release prophetic words, the Holy Spirit would test me. He expanded my faith and made me trust Him when I prophesied. He took me from knowing what I would say to trusting Him to provide the words as I approached someone to release a word to them.

Years later He tested me again. He instructed me not to write one sermon for six months but allow Him to speak to me every time I got up to the pulpit, even if I didn't have one piece of direction from Him until a minute before I was to start preaching. I remember thinking more than once, "Holy Spirit, are You late? Are You going to show up? I'm walking up to the pulpit, and the first sentence is still not appearing." Yet He always showed up—and still does. I learned to trust. To this day, I don't write sermons because He can preach through me out of the overflow of the Spirit and the Word of God I have stored up within.

It's Time for Activation

You can walk in the prophetic too. Begin to receive the Holy Spirit in His fullness and trust Him.

Prayer of Repentance, Renunciation, and Breaking Agreement

Jesus, please forgive me for not embracing my destiny. I receive the calling and anointing You have placed on my life. I renounce and break agreement with stubbornness, self-will, and pride. I command anything blocking my destiny to be released now in Jesus' name. I lay down my flesh for Your will, Lord. I trust You with my life and destiny. I want to be powerful for the kingdom of God. I ask for Your forgiveness, and I forgive myself. In Jesus' name, amen.

Impartation and Activation Prayer

Holy Spirit, come upon me now! I ask to receive the Spirit of God in fullness with both fire and power. I desire every gift to manifest, and I call forth the baptism of fire and power with evidence of all the gifts. I believe I receive it. Holy Spirit, come and fill me to overflowing. Fill me with Your love and Spirit. I proclaim I will walk in my prophetic destiny and exude the power of God at all times. Holy Spirit, fill me afresh. Where I have faltered or felt dry and stagnant, give me fresh fire! Baptize me afresh in Your love, Spirit, and fire! In Jesus' name, amen.

Prophetic Proclamations (Faith Declarations)

I speak and pronounce that I walk in and release the prophetic fluently and uninhibited.

I release the raw power of the Holy Spirit to come forth through my life to impact and reach others for the kingdom of God.

I summon my prophetic destiny to full manifestation. I put prophetic demand on the spiritual realm to activate and materialize my prophetic words.

I call forth prophetic words to be fulfilled in my life. I speak and decree the spiritual realm moves and activates on my behalf.

I declare I have faith, and I trust the Holy Spirit with the discernment I receive.

Spiritual Activation

Activate the prophetic! Try these three exercises to activate the prophetic within you.

1. Practice getting a word of knowledge or wisdom. Give a cashier or waitress a compliment and then focus on the Holy Spirit and see whether He would give you a word or picture to release in addition to the natural compliment. Expect to receive something to release spiritually.
2. Meditate and spend time in silence. Ask the Holy Spirit to speak to you. Journal about what you received. Keep writing down in the next season what you hear in your mind and spirit, and see whether you can identify when the Spirit of the Lord is speaking clearly.
3. Discern your prophetic words. Seek the Holy Spirit for creative strategies and declarative prayer word choices to call forth to see the fulfillment of your words.

Spiritual Warfare Declarations

I disperse every evil attack against my life, and I command these attacks to dissipate in Jesus' name.

I incinerate and burn up completely every demonic blueprint written in the spiritual realm with my name on it.

I restrain demonic infiltrations from coming against my blessings and inheritance.

In the name of Jesus I bind from activation every evil perpetrator causing illegal and harmful attacks in the spiritual realm because of my destiny. I restrict your activities by the blood of the Lamb.

In Jesus' name I evict and expel every demonic assignment of sabotage and spirit of abortion sent to steal, kill, and destroy my prophecies and destiny.

Chapter 3

SPIRITUAL CLEANSING AND PROTECTION

When my husband and I had been married for five years, our house was robbed. The burglar staked out our home while we were having a garage sale. The police investigators said the man probably walked in the back door when we were busy with guests, staked out whether our house was worth plundering, and walked out the front door. A few days later, he entered our home through our bedroom window about an hour after we left for work. He knew we were gone, so he stayed for a while and helped himself to a soda and a forty-five-minute premium entertainment call.

We felt invaded and defiled. But we left our back door open, and it gave him a right to invade. Not only did we leave our back door open the day of the garage sale, we also failed to lock our garage the day he broke in, enabling him to obtain a tool to pry open our unlocked bedroom window. I now know that when you have a garage sale, you should lock all windows and doors to your house. Give no place to the enemy. (See Ephesians 4:27.)

The devil also comes in and tries to rob us. The burglar was able to rob our home because we had no security system; we had no alarm and let down our guard. Remember, the enemy comes to steal, kill, and destroy (John 10:10), especially after we have done ministry or have had a prophetic breakthrough. He wants to steal your destiny, rob your health, and bankrupt your finances. He is out to steal, kill, and destroy your life, your children, and your business, and he will use any means necessary to keep you from accomplishing God's purpose.

This is why it is so important to close the door to demonic backlash and stay spiritually strong. The Bible describes the enemy as a thief. Like a thief, he can infiltrate through your back door—a door of your soul he enters when you are unaware. You might be focused in a particular direction, completely unaware that he seeks to invade your soul and release a warfare attack when you least expect it.

The challenge with the enemy coming in our back door is we don't see it, the way I didn't see the robber enter the back door of my house. Therefore, the robber got to come back and plunder my goods. The enemy also plunders our goods. The goods he plunders are our emotions, health, and self-worth. He wants us to feel defeated and unworthy, and he wants to leave us in condemnation, feeling stuck and unable to move forward.

When the enemy comes in the back door, we often don't know we have been attacked until days, weeks, or months later, when we suddenly experience something we haven't dealt with before. We might feel rejected when rejection never bothered us. We might feel pain in our bodies even though we didn't injure ourselves. We might worry or be fearful about things where we previously had trust and security.

We discover the backdoor attack as we are quickened prophetically in our senses. Our souls and spirits can alert us that something is off as we start to discern and analyze why we feel fine one day and then experience something uncommon the next day. We can be quickened and alerted by unusual happenings.

Engaging in spiritual warfare and doing kingdom ministry paints a bull's-eye target on you. The enemy will oppose the advancement you are doing for the kingdom of God. You have to be alert and aware of his tactics. He will put up resistance. When you know his deployments and patterns against you, it will empower you to fight victoriously on the offense, not the defense.

Writing this manuscript has released great warfare in my life. I know the enemy doesn't want people mobilized to subdue spiritual darkness, so the resistance is intense—but we are more than overcomers in Christ Jesus.

> No, in all these things we are more than conquerors through Him who loved us. For I am persuaded that neither death nor life, neither angels nor principalities nor powers, neither things present nor things to come, neither height nor depth, nor any other created thing, shall be able to separate us from the love of God, which is in Christ Jesus our Lord.
>
> —Romans 8:37–39

God's love is enough to crush what the enemy throws our way. Our focus should be on the finished work of the cross and staying strong to complete the mission He has set before us. When Jesus went to the cross, He didn't give up, and neither should we.

How do you stay spiritually strong, cleansed, and protected while you accomplish God's call on your life? Develop a battle plan of action to help you guard your heart, close demonic access, and bind and restrict the enemy on the offense. You are probably familiar with the home security system called ADT (American District Telegraph). I like to apply this familiar acronym to my spiritual security system and pray against ungodly *A=attachments, D=defilements, or T=transferences.* When I am done with a ministry event or deliverance session, I always pray and put my security system in place by decreeing in Jesus' name that there will be no ungodly attachments, defilements, or transferences.

I further pray and speak out, "There will be no retribution from the enemy for the work of the Lord I did and for the deliverance of the captives. I speak and decree that the blood of the Lamb covers my family, children, finances, pets, home, vehicles, ministry, and health. I ask God to dispatch angels to guard and protect everything and to refresh me." Now, I am not legalistic about this, but I do pray this as led by the Spirit, and as I feel I should establish a firewall around myself and those I love.

Prophetic Exercise: Pray a Firewall of Protection

Pray with me now! Speak audibly!

Holy Spirit, I thank You for the knowledge I am receiving. I command there will be no retribution for learning how to wage prophetic spiritual warfare. I speak and decree the blood of the Lamb covers my family, children, finances, pets, appliances, home, vehicles, ministry, and health. I speak and decree that no weapon formed against me will prosper. Send forth Your angels to guard and protect everyone I love and all my assets. I come against spirits of confusion. I speak clarity and understanding as I study this topic. I bind every evil ruler from sending forth attacks and hindering my destiny.

I speak and decree that there will be no backlash. I command my prophetic words to be released according to the will of God. In Jesus' name, amen!

Relationship With the Father

I want to talk about your relationship with God. What name do you call God? I am not talking about Jesus or the Holy Spirit. I am talking about the ultimate person of the Trinity, Father God. Take a moment and identify the name you use to address God. Your terminology in addressing God reveals where you are in your walk with Him and the place of intimacy you hold with Him. God is Father. Father is personal and intimate.

Prophetic Exercise: Identify God as Father

If you have never addressed God as Father in your prayer time or vocabulary, I want you to stop right here and meditate on a few things. Did you have a breach in a relationship with your earthly father? Did he ever say, "I love you"? Was he nice or mean and aggressive? Did he ever abuse you? Did he abandon you? Our earthly father relationship has a direct impact on our heavenly Father relationship. Please seek soul healing if you have father issues. My book *Unshackled* will assist you to receive inner healing and deliverance in your soul.

Sexual defilement is another factor that can block our relationship with our heavenly Father. Sadly it is all too common an issue, and yet many people don't realize it at first. If people have been abused or fondled inappropriately, it's common to stuff those feelings and block out those experiences. The problem is they still create trauma, causing a need for emotional healing and possibly deliverance from demonic spirits. I have ministered to many Christians who didn't think they were sexually abused in any way. After we went through several sessions, the Holy Spirit would reveal the abuse. They didn't have to relive it; they needed to recognize and heal from it. There can be issues in our pasts—even though we are unaware of them—that can still be active in the spiritual realm over us that must be dealt with and removed. It was a sign of maturity that they were ready to handle what was in their past and get free from it.

Have you been sexually abused? Not everyone has. However, if your answer is no, I ask you to meditate further on this question and take it to the Holy Spirit. Think back if there was ever a time someone touched you inappropriately, but you shrugged it off or didn't think much of it. Were you uncomfortable with the way someone looked at you or touched you? Don't let this opportunity pass you by. Think back right now and determine whether something comes to remembrance through this prophetic exercise.

Prophetic Exercise:
Freedom From Abuse

Was there ever a time someone touched you inappropriately or that you were sexually assaulted? Can you remember a moment you were uncomfortable with something someone did no matter how minuscule? If you can easily remember something, you may need healing if you have not already received it. Think of the situation and focus on what kind of feelings it brings forth. Do not overthink it or try to relive the situation. Do you need to release forgiveness toward an offender or a family member for not preventing these actions? What do you feel? How can you release those feelings?

If your answer is still no, based on my experience as a deliverance minister, I want to take you one step deeper.

Prophetic Exercise: Holy Spirit Revelation

Pray and ask the Holy Spirit to reveal anything hidden or in the dark from your past. (See Mark 4:22.) I press this issue because I want to lead you to freedom. I've seen people ignore it or not allow the Spirit in to receive complete deliverance. I've witnessed the benefits of the transformation. I praise God if you haven't experienced it, but I ask you to be honest enough with yourself and the Lord to allow Him to search you and reveal all things, not just the things you choose. The attitude of "what you don't know won't hurt you" *does* hurt you. As you mature in your walk with the Lord, and as He releases revelation to you, it leads to freedom.

Trust the Holy Spirit to reveal it and release it in His time. When you feel He is convicting you and bringing you back to this memory, proceed with this exercise.

Quiet yourself and ask the Holy Spirit to reveal and bring into the light anything that is hidden that He wants to reveal to lead to healing. If the Holy Spirit brings something forth, pray into it and trust Him to lead you through the healing process. Don't allow the devil a foothold. Bind and restrict vain imaginations and false scenarios. Trust that the Holy Spirit is a gentleman, and if He needs to bring anything forth, He will do so in love and dignity. He will not reveal things to cause you trauma, fear, or hurt, unless it is to lead you to and through deliverance. The end result of what you discover should bring forth fruit in your life and ultimately give you peace and glorify the name of Jesus Christ.

I genuinely believe that if a person has been abused but doesn't remember it, the Holy Spirit will reveal it in the right time. He knows when each person can handle it. I have witnessed many Christians who discovered their abuse and were thankful they did. Now that they have been set free from the trauma and associated soul ties, they feel differently about themselves. It has changed their lives!

After you remove these roadblocks—you receive healing from any issues with your earthly father or any sexual abuse—you will be able to come into a tight relationship with the heavenly Father. People don't address Him as Father because they don't know Him as Father. To know Him as Father, you must remove things from your past that prevent you from becoming close to Him. When we get close to Him, we will see Him as a loving Father who will never hurt us but will only have our best interests in mind. You will notice changes in your vocabulary and adornment of Father God as you increase the intensity of your relationship with Him and you begin saying, "Father," when referring to Him.

Stay in a Place of Rest

Wrestling against dark forces and being spiritually attacked can wear on you physically, emotionally, and spiritually. Staying in a place of perpetual rest with the heavenly Father is crucial when you are on the front lines of battle. When you are with your Father, nothing will be impenetrable. When a weapon or dart from the enemy tries to invade your soul, you will be so full of the presence of the Lord that you can dismiss it easily.

Being in a place of rest is relaxing. Enjoy His presence and ease your mind from the struggles. Rest is not warfare prayer. It is a time to fill up and not pour out. There is a time to release the anointing and a time to be refreshed.

Enjoying the presence of the Lord is difficult for people because we are accustomed to being continually active and having to work for things. It challenges us to settle down our minds and our physical bodies to rest. I have had seasons when I can't get enough rest in Him, and I never want another day without this kind of peace and impartation. Other times, I am so busy that taking the time to be still and rest, even for a few minutes, is a challenge. Yet it feels so good to be protected in that place of peace and oneness with Him. Rest refreshes you and gives you the strength to keep going.

How do we rest in His presence? We quiet our minds and wait to receive from Him. One way to do this is to play soft worship, prophetic, instrumental, or soaking music. I choose to prostrate myself most of the time when I listen to music to get refreshed in His presence. There is something about humbling yourself and going to the floor that I enjoy. I put a notepad close by for revelation I may receive or to quickly write down a distracting thought on a to-do list. This way, I can put it out of my mind without worrying that I will forget it later. Resting in His presence is glorious and necessary as we learn how to be victorious over spiritual warfare.

Establishing boundaries in your life is important. We must know the limits of what we can handle and step back when we begin to get overloaded. Boundaries need to be established with family, work, ministry, and everything! Establishing safe limits and a balance of peace, work, ministry, and "God time" makes us better ministers, employees, bosses, spouses, parents, and friends. Learning to say no or stop—in other words, establishing healthy boundaries—can help us remove demonic access points.

When you become worn down, the enemy gains a foothold in your life. When you live a busy life with many demands, you are not as alert as you should be, and the enemy can use those opportunities to come in your back door. We can also experience mental fatigue, which is an access point to our souls. Our guards are down when we experience pressure and fatigue. We can become consumed with our problems, the drought on our lives, and the defeat we feel. When this happens, we will not be in prayer as we should. Therefore, we aren't as discerning as we need to be.

CLOSE THE BACK DOOR

The thief comes in when we are not watching, which is why the Bible tells us to be alert and vigilant. "Be sober and watchful, because your adversary the devil walks around as a roaring lion, seeking whom he may devour" (1 Pet. 5:8). One way the enemy has gained access in my life is during times I have ministered deliverance to others. I have learned that when I am done ministering, I must spend time in prayer. I pray against the spiritual backlash, ask God to dispatch angels on assignment, and rest in the Father.

Jesus went alone to be with the Father after He ministered. Follow Jesus' example. It will keep you in a place of rest and in a place where enemy access is denied. The devil is seeking loopholes in your life. One of those loopholes is to do ministry when you are in a struggle. You can go through things, and yes, God can use you, but when you are going through an enormous battle, it is best to withdraw and retreat for a time of consecration and refocus. Consecration is a time dedicated to and focused on the Lord through prayer, fasting, and solitude. Experiencing intense warfare can cause you to focus on the physical warfare at hand and not necessarily on what is unseen. That which is unseen penetrates and enters your back door and leaves you worse off than before.

Repent quickly to close any entry points to sin and keep the enemy from entering your back door. Seek God for your breakthrough. Pressing through to your deliverance breaks passivity and stagnancy, and as those things are broken off your life, the enemy is exposed and removed. It doesn't mean you need to see a demon around every corner. It means you need to be alert and open to the possibility that evil spirits could be lurking. Discovering what is your flesh and what is demonic will assist you in knowing how to pray precisely.

Pray on the Offense

A good place to start winning the battle against the enemy is to pray on the offense and not the defense. Forceful, fierce, and authoritative prayers annihilate the enemy's camp and plunder his goods against you. Believe in faith that when you collaborate with the Holy Spirit, He will give you adequate words to speak. Develop a close personal relationship with the Holy Spirit that includes partnering with Him in prayer—not just praying in tongues but joining forces and praying with Him in your native language.

Rely on the Holy Spirit when you pray. "Likewise, the Spirit helps us in our weaknesses, for we do not know what to pray for as we ought, but the Spirit Himself intercedes for us with groanings too deep for words" (Rom. 8:26). Our prayer lives become stagnant because we are bored with our prayer lives. Involve the Holy Spirit and allow Him to pray through you.

This will cause your prayer time to become vibrant and full of life. It will be so fun that you won't want to stop praying! This type of collaboration with the Holy Spirit begins by developing a relationship, listening, and trusting.

Cleansing From Past Wounds

Spiritual cleansing begins with us. My husband says, "If you want to see revival, draw a circle on the ground and take one step forward and put yourself in it." Before we can deliver the world, we must seek deliverance. Soul wounds are open entry points to the demonic realm. We must remove these entry points to protect ourselves. Inner healing and deliverance go hand in hand. You cannot have one without the other. Inner healing is discovering our soul wounds, releasing and receiving forgiveness, and working through our feelings and thoughts about the attacks, wounds, and abuses we have suffered. Deliverance is casting out the correlating demonic spirit when applicable.

Inner healing will bring peace to our souls. The devil doesn't want us to keep that peace, and demonic attacks and spiritual strongholds are some of the ways he tries to steal our peace. When we have dealt with generational curses, soul wounds, abuses, and other afflictions for years, they can become strongholds in our lives. Through adverse situations, emotions, and circumstances—even such things as accidents, addictions, and near-death experiences—demonic spirits can infiltrate our souls and must be cast out. When we don't receive breakthrough, it is often because we received inner healing but didn't go deep enough to cast out the correlating demonic spirit as Jesus did. When we don't allow inner healing and deliverance to manifest together, we receive temporary relief but not lasting results. Evil spirits need to be cast out in order to seal in our inner healing and have it come forth to full completion. In my book *Unshackled* I discuss this further and lead people to and through inner healing and deliverance. (See the appendix.)

When we are not spiritually cleansed, demonic access points and evil spirits can attack us. How can we effectively wage war if, inside us, we harbor the very thing we are attempting to combat in the spirit realm? I remember a prime example of this. My team and I were conducting a deliverance session, and one team member had a spirit of anger that hadn't been completely evicted. We were ministering to a person who had a strong spirit of anger. As my team tried to cast out the person's anger, the team member with a spirit of anger began to manifest. We had to remove the team member from the session so there wouldn't be interference with the person's deliverance.

Enemy Intelligence

The enemy knows your struggles and weaknesses. He has observed generational curses and has sent forth monitoring spirits. He knows how to push your buttons because he sees what upsets you and triggers you to go off in a negative direction. He knows how you struggle and what consumes you.

The words we speak are powerful and release things into the spiritual atmosphere. The enemy wants to wreak havoc on your life. As the enemy gathers intelligence on your life, new warfare attacks arise and manifest. Years ago the Lord revealed to me how to pray effectively against the information the enemy gathers. The demonic world uses communication lines and frequency channels in the spiritual realm.

Prophetic Exercise: Declarations Against Spiritual Attack

Here are a few declarations from my book *Discerning and Destroying the Works of Satan* that the Holy Spirit supernaturally gave to me. Use these as examples of what to speak out loud, and refer to that book for the full revelation and list of declarations that you can pray out against attacks in your life.

- In Jesus' name I command demonic guards and territorial spirits not to follow, hear, report back, or gather information to use against me.
- I dissolve and desecrate evil communication currents and frequency channels in the spiritual realm with the blood of the Lamb.
- I command demonic troops to be disassembled, dismantled, disobedient, unorganized, and uncommitted to their assignments.
- I send interference into the enemy's camp to destroy his organizational tactics.
- I bind all spiritual chatter and silence the mouth of the adversary and his cohorts. In Jesus' name I command all chatter dispatched against me, my family, and my ministry to stop immediately.

Fear of Evil Spirits

There is nothing to fear when thinking about evil spirits. Jesus said, "Look, I give you authority to trample on serpents and scorpions, and over all the power of the enemy. And nothing shall by any means hurt you" (Luke 10:19). We have authority over the devil; he doesn't have authority over us. He may throw a spiritual attack your way, but the power of God within you has the final say.

Like I said earlier, the Bible doesn't say we will never be attacked. It says the attack won't prosper. "No weapon that is formed against you shall prosper" (Isa. 54:17). The Complete Jewish Bible says, "No weapon made will prevail against you." *Prevail* means to be effective or effectual. *Effective* means to produce a desired effect. We cannot argue when we study the prophetic layers of this verse. It could read: "No weapon or attack formed against you will be effective or produce the enemy's desired results. Instead, any weapon that comes your way will be refuted by the Lord."

We see a story of demonic manifestations in Mark 5. "But when he saw Jesus afar off, he ran up and kneeled before Him, and cried out with a loud voice, 'What have You to do with me, Jesus, Son of the Most High God? I adjure You by God, do not torment me'" (vv. 6–7). The demons are afraid of Jesus and cry out loudly, begging Him not to torment them. Demons are afraid of the power of God. We have the power of God inside us through the indwelling power of the Holy Spirit. Therefore, the demons should fear the Spirit of God in us, and we shouldn't be afraid.

I remember once when I was in a remote location for ministry, and I could see the demons in that place. I make it a habit to play recorded Scripture to cleanse the atmosphere when I am in a new place or hotel room. Therefore, I set up my iPod on my dock to play Scripture. I listened to it while I unpacked, and then I left the room to visit with my host. When I returned, the dock and iPod were separated and scattered on the other side of the room. I had only been gone for a couple of hours, but I was nearby the entire time, close enough to know no one had entered the room. In spite of these events, I slept in that room, and I was not afraid. I know I go in the name of the Lord, and I know my God is greater than every evil spirit.

It's Time for Activation

Close the door to the enemy, and enter the perfect rest of your relationship with God.

Prayer of Repentance, Renunciation, and Breaking Agreement

Jesus, I ask for Your forgiveness, and I repent of any uncleanness, impurity, and sin to which I have contributed. I break agreement with sin that was an open doorway for demonic infiltration in my home, spiritual life, emotions, and relationship with You. I repent of any ungodly actions and thoughts. I repent for not closing the door to the enemy in all areas of my life. I ask You to forgive me for any distance in our relationship. I destroy every stronghold I have come into agreement with and command it to leave now in Jesus' name. Amen.

Impartation and Activation Prayer

Jesus, give me a strong desire to be in Your presence. Where I have been disobedient and lacked discipline, give me perseverance, drive, and desire. Lord, I love You, and I want to grow closer to You. Remove everything that is not of You, including possessions, friendships, idols, and behavior patterns and habits. Help me to seek You with everything in me and give You first priority in my life. I receive Your love and ask You, Holy Spirit, to remove roadblocks and hindrances. Help me be productive and fruitful in my day and spiritual walk. I trust You to love me and know You will never hurt me. In Jesus' name, amen!

Prophetic Proclamations (Faith Declarations)

I proclaim that I am loved by the Father, and I have an intimate relationship with Him with no hindrances or obstacles.

I decree that my spiritual walk increases and that I go from glory to glory. The presence of the Lord surrounds me.

I cancel any hindering spirit that would try to prevent angels from carrying out their assignment to guard and protect my family and me. I speak and declare that I am covered with the blood of Jesus, and no weapon formed against me will prosper.

I say that I am a worshipper. I love to worship and spend my free time worshipping the Father in spirit, truth, and freedom.

I proclaim that my earthly relationships in no way inhibit my relationship with my heavenly Father, His Son Jesus, and the Holy Spirit.

Spiritual Activation

1. Pray and anoint your home, vehicle, possessions, and bank accounts. Pray for protection around everything you own and everyone important to you, including family members and pets.
2. Develop a plan to increase your spiritual walk, and seek deliverance from Jesus. Allow the Holy Spirit to lead and guide you through a productive time of intimacy with the Trinity.
3. Receive deliverance from any father wounds or sexual abuse you may have experienced. Find a trusted deliverance minister, and work through the issues that hold you back from fully receiving the Father's love.

Spiritual Warfare Declarations

I bind and restrict every demonic operation from coming against my destiny. In the name of Jesus I speak to every distraction and delay in my life, and I command you to cease! You are restricted from activating against me.

I speak and decree that the plans of time stealers and destiny wasters on assignment from the kingdom of darkness are diffused.

In Jesus' name I abort every demonic deployment and mission that would come against the building and enhancement of my relationship with the Lord.

I expel and forcefully eject every monitoring spirit sent to disrupt my spiritual growth.

I annihilate with the fire of God every evil ploy against my faith and against increase in my relationship with the Lord.

Chapter 4

SPIRITUAL WARFARE IS AUDIBLE

We've all heard that the battle is in our minds. But have we heard that the victory comes out of our mouths? Our words are prophetically assigned and targeted to get results. Visualize your words coming out as a forceful stream of air going across the room. They hit a target and get results. We are hosts of the Ruach Ha'Kodesh, the breath of God, and since He has given us dominion when we speak, it is His breath, His words, and the spiritual realm must respond.

There is power in the words we speak, even if we don't know it or believe it! My son-in-law knew when he started to date my daughter that he wanted to marry her. He didn't know the power of his words, but he kept declaring, and it manifested. My daughter would declare out she would have a horse and a dog, and it manifested. The power of our words can go in both a positive and negative direction. Proverbs 18:21 says, "Death and life are in the power of the tongue." Our words can activate and call things forth and bind and restrict the enemy.

The principle to bind and loose needs to be done audibly. "I will give you the keys of the kingdom of heaven, and whatever you bind on earth shall be bound in heaven, and whatever you loose on earth shall be loosed in heaven" (Matt. 16:19). The demonic realm cannot hear what you pray when you pray silently, connecting your spirit man to the Holy Spirit. You take authority over the demonic realm when you speak out—when you decree and declare using your voice.

Our heavenly Father spoke out when He created the earth in Genesis 1, and Jesus spoke out on several occasions in the Gospels when He prayed for healing to come forth and demons to flee. David additionally called and cried out to God for deliverance. David *cried*, *called*, and *said*. These words are verbs and indicate action. The words also mean an audible plea. *Cried* in these scriptures does not refer to shedding tears but making a loud plea for God to stop the warfare and deliver him from his enemies. We should fight warfare the way the Bible models it: audibly.

Jesus Spoke Out

Jesus modeled how He fought the devil when He was tempted in the wilderness. He answered by quoting the Word—by saying, "It is written."

> But He answered, "It is written, 'Man shall not live by bread alone, but by every word that proceeds out of the mouth of God.'"
>
> —Matthew 4:4

> Jesus said to him, "It is also written, 'You shall not tempt the Lord your God.'"
>
> —Matthew 4:7

> Then Jesus said to him, "Get away from here, Satan! For it is written, 'You shall worship the Lord your God, and Him only shall you serve.'"
>
> —Matthew 4:10

Jesus said. *The American Dictionary of the English Language* defines the word *say* as to speak, utter in words, declare, confess, and pronounce.[1] These are audible actions that we speak out with our voices and mouths. Jesus fought the devil, not by thinking the Word of God but by speaking out the Word of God. He additionally spoke out when He ministered in healing and deliverance. He constantly spoke to things. He spoke to a demon and said, "Be silent and come out of him!" (Mark 1:25); He spoke to a fig tree (Mark 11:14); He said to a leper, "Be clean" (Matt. 8:3); and He told a paralyzed man to take up his bed and walk (Mark 2:11). Jesus modeled audible spiritual warfare and demonstrated the power and authority of the spoken word.

Jesus was in the ministry of deliverance. He knew how to bind and restrict the enemy and cast out demons. When we study the Gospels, we can see that Jesus fought warfare audibly and spoke out commands to make demons leave.

> "Be silent and come out of him!" (Mark 1:25).
>
> "Come out of the man, you unclean spirit!" (Mark 5:8).
>
> "You mute and deaf spirit, I command you, come out of him, and enter him no more" (Mark 9:25).

The devil is not omniscient (infinitely knowing; all-seeing), omnipotent (possessing unlimited power), or omnipresent (present in all places at the same time). Therefore, he cannot hear your thoughts or what you silently pray when you connect your spirit to the Holy Spirit. One time, I taught a person how to rebuke the enemy, and he kept rebuking the enemy in his mind. What he prayed for never manifested, and a natural physical intervention was required in his situation instead of divine supernatural intervention from heaven.

We are uncomfortable and unfamiliar with audible prayers and declarations because before many of us entered Spirit-filled churches, we weren't taught to pray out loud to bind and restrict the spiritual realm or call forth the blessings of God. We aren't confident, and we worry about what our prayers will sound like when we begin to speak out. Therefore, we stay silent and try to fight the enemy in our minds instead of out of our mouths, and we don't get the results we desire.

Here's a prime example. You are gathered at a meal, and it's time to bless the food. What happens? There's an awkward pause as everyone hopes someone else will volunteer to pray aloud. If there's a pastor in the group, everyone defers to him or her. They are intimidated to pray audibly for fear of what others will think and what it will sound like.

We are not afraid to shout at the TV, scream at a football game, tell someone off, or cheer someone on. We need not be concerned with what it will look like or sound like if we pray out loud, take authority, and, yes, even sometimes shout at the devil.

Who knows? You might get some freedom if you yell at the enemy and put him under your feet. If he isn't under your feet, it's because you don't put him there with the power of your words.

Prophetic Exercise: Declare Audibly Against the Enemy

What do you need to take authority over? Where do you need to put the devil under your feet? Speak out, right now! Use the following declarations to get you started, and then have faith as you begin to declare audibly that the Holy Spirit will partner with you and reveal what needs to be spoken aloud for your situation.

> I bind and restrict every demonic assignment against my family, my health, and my finances. I command your attacks to cease to exist. Get out of here and exit my premises. Cease and desist of every assignment against me and those I love and care about. I proclaim no weapon formed against us will prosper (Isa. 54:17).
>
> Every evil attack against my mind, every infiltrating spirit trying to attack me with fear, trauma, anxiety, depression, mental illness, defeat, and victim mentality, I tell you to abort your assignment. You are restricted from having access to my mind. I have a sound, self-disciplined, and self-controlled mind (2 Tim. 1:7). I proclaim I have the mind of Christ (1 Cor. 2:16).
>
> Every demonic intrusion into my generational line and coming against my prophetic words, I rebuke, cancel, and nullify your effects in the spiritual realm. I speak and decree that my destiny will go forth without hindrance, delay, or destruction. Every demonic marker with my name assigned to it, I burn up your point of contact and marker with the fire of God. The fire of God apprehends my enemies and brings forth generational blessing and my prophetic destiny!

We must be forceful against the enemy, using the authority Jesus gives us as we speak out against the powers of darkness. The Bible says, "And from the days of John the Baptist until now the kingdom of heaven suffers violence, and the violent take it by force" (Matt. 11:12, NKJV). The Modern English Version translates the same verse as, "From the days of John the Baptist until now, the kingdom of heaven has forcefully advanced, and the strong take it by force." We need to be forceful and strong with the power of our words. Our words are prophetically assigned and targeted to create a spiritual result. We want to create a result when we bind and restrict the enemy against us. We accomplish this when we speak out our prayers into the spiritual realm so that the demonic realm must respond to the words we speak and the authority we exude.

Pray in the Natural

Spiritual warfare prayers can be prayed in the natural by what we know about a situation. We can apply destructive words to the spiritual realm by taking natural knowledge we have about a situation and praying to destroy the powers of darkness against us. We know circumstances and what specific prayers and words we can target in that direction. We all have a level of intelligence and common sense of what needs to be prayed. It's effective to pray in the natural until the spiritual kicks in, but we should aim to go deeper, further, and wider in our prayer lives. Prayer is the foundation. Establishing a foundation in the natural will assist us as we transition into the spiritual.

The Scripture is a great place to gain information and wisdom on what needs to be prophetically spoken through prayer. The Book of Psalms is a prayer book and a great place to stock our arsenals with artillery against the devil. The Bible is a phenomenal tool against the devil and evil spirits in every situation we encounter. In your Bible underline or highlight prayers, warfare scriptures, and powerful weaponry you can use against the devil in your prayer time. I additionally label each psalm as praise, warfare, or a specific topic that describes them for easy cross-reference. This practice helps me to have them readily available at a moment's notice when I need to speak out against a particular situation.

The Holy Spirit Is Your Guide

Stagnancy and dryness can hit your prayer life. You pray and fall asleep or get bored, feeling like you always pray the same repetitive prayers. Have you ever considered the Holy Spirit as your Guide in your prayer time? "But when the Spirit of truth comes, He will guide you into all truth. For He will not speak on His own authority. But He will speak whatever He hears" (John 16:13).

The Holy Spirit is connected to God the Father and Jesus, His Son. Jesus is our great intercessor, and the Holy Spirit is here to assist us. Do we tap into His assistance through prayer? In this particular example of prayer, I am not speaking about praying in tongues, although what I will teach you could be applied to when you pray in tongues.

We can pray in the natural based on what we know, and we can incorporate scriptures into our prayer time. But what about inviting the Holy Spirit into our prayer time? The prophetic in prophetic spiritual warfare is to let the Holy Spirit lead and guide. We have the Holy Spirit dwelling inside of us. You need to tap into His power and mindfully focus on your spirit man and the Holy Spirit when you pray. Co-labor with the Holy Spirit in prayer, and it will help you pray what the Holy Spirit knows needs to be prayed, called forth, and released into the spiritual realm. The Holy Spirit knows best because He is part of the Trinity, the greatest team of three.

How do we partner with the Spirit in prayer? Begin to pray in the natural. Pray what you know, feel, or think. Speak out scriptures. Think about how you best connect with the Lord. You may need to get in a place of quiet, peace, or worship to tap into or stir the presence of God. Positioning yourself to connect your spirit man to the Holy Spirit is instrumental in co-laboring with the Spirit of God.

As you desire to tap into the power of the Spirit within you, stop thinking about what you are doing (praying) and trust that the Holy Spirit will speak through you. Build a deep relationship with the Holy Spirit; it will help you trust Him to guide you in what to pray. As you begin to release natural prayer and trust the Holy Spirit to collaborate with you in prayer, He will start to give you words of knowledge and unction in the spirit of what needs to be prayed. You may see a picture, you may hear a word, or something will arise within you to pray in a specific direction. Follow His lead and trust Him to give you precise direction about what needs to be prayed.

Bind and restrict distracting thoughts. Don't allow your mind to wander. You have inside you the same power that raised Jesus Christ from the dead: the Holy Spirit. Tap into that power source. Trust that He will give you the words to pray and will lead and guide you. This is how you pray prophetically led by the Spirit of God.

Focus your attention on the Holy Spirit while praying. This will help you to receive revelation. As we receive revelation, it becomes an impartation that leads to application. While we pray, we not only want to annihilate the forces of darkness, but we seek prayer strategies that will help us pray more effectively. When the Holy Spirit gives us prophetic insight into the spiritual realm, we can further discern that information to target our prayers in a specific direction for desired results.

Ignite Your Prayer Life

Begin your prayer time with worship, because this moves you into the presence of God. As you experience the presence of God, you get caught up in the things of God. Peace and joy will come upon you. It seems that when you and I get caught up in the presence of the Lord, the cares of this world subside. As cares subside, your mind closes down, and you stop thinking and analyzing everything. As you connect your spirit to His Spirit, you can communicate openly and freely with Him. Revelation will come forth, and soon you will discover what you pray in the natural has transitioned to spiritual prayer.

Let me explain that a little further. When you pray in the natural, your mind is praying, and you think about what to pray next and may stumble over your words or even feel stagnant or bored, as I said before. When you connect your spirit to the Holy Spirit, suddenly what you pray in the natural transitions to the spiritual, and your prayer life becomes energized. As your prayer life is exhilarated, it becomes fun to pray because the Holy Ghost pours out through you, and suddenly you don't want to stop praying.

This is the very point we want to get to, whether we bind and restrict the demonic realm or call and command blessings and positive things to come forth. We need the Holy Spirit to change and charge us so much that we want to stay in our prayer closets and intertwine our spirits to His Spirit through prayer. Try it now. Put this book aside, and begin to pray in the natural for a specific situation that hasn't received an answer or breakthrough.

Prophetic Exercise: Allow the Holy Spirit to Lead Your Prayer

Invite the Holy Spirit into your prayer time right now. Begin to praise God. Don't give Him your prayer list. Praise and adore Him with words. Now transition to what you feel needs to be prayed, using discernment and perception. Allow the Holy Spirit to tell your spirit what needs to be prayed. You could say, "Holy Spirit, please lead me in my prayer time. I invite You in and yield to Your direction. Reveal strategies and the words to pray out of my spirit man. I trust You for what You want to reveal and release."

Often we read about ways to empower our prayer lives but never apply them. That's why I hope you participated in the prophetic exercise above. I want you to stop and do it now. I'm passionate about it because I know it will help you discover a new way to pray and tap into the ultimate power source to manifest your prayers.

It's Time for Activation

The Holy Spirit is ready to change you and ignite your prayers. Let's activate this power in your life.

Prayer of Repentance, Renunciation, and Breaking Agreement

Heavenly Father, I repent for prayerlessness. I'm sorry for times when I should have been more active in my prayer life. I break agreement with laziness and settling for less than what You have for me. I command condemnation to not come upon me but for conviction from the Holy Spirit to call me into action. I renounce stagnancy in my prayer life and spiritual walk. I speak and decree a change and turnaround in Jesus' name. Amen!

IMPARTATION AND ACTIVATION PRAYER

Holy Spirit, I ask You to convict me and correct me in my prayer time. I invite You in my prayer time to be my leader, guide, and friend. Instruct me on what and how to pray. Lead me along in the pathway of truth. Help me to hear Your voice. I rely on and trust in You. Help me to go to deeper places in my prayer time as I enhance my prayer life. Convict me to pray audibly and speak to the spiritual realm. Guide me in my prayer time when I am praying silently and I should transition to audible prayer. In Jesus' name, amen.

PROPHETIC PROCLAMATIONS (FAITH DECLARATIONS)

I am not stagnant in my prayer life and spiritual walk. I grow daily and am spiritually strong.

I call forth a deeper relationship with the Holy Spirit. I proclaim that I will tap into the Holy Spirit in my prayer time and partner with Him.

I decree and declare I will set aside time daily to seek the presence of the Lord and hear from the Holy Spirit in prayer.

Spiritual warfare is audible; therefore, I will speak out and decree into the spiritual realm to bind and restrict the enemy. I will not be stagnant or passive in my prayer time.

I confess I will arise and take my authority in my prayer time. I have a mouth, and I will use it to advance the kingdom of God and bind and restrict the enemy from further attacks.

Spiritual Activation

1. Transition your prayer time to audible prayer. If you have prayed silently for years, try to pray audibly. Allow the Holy Spirit to lead and guide you when to speak out and when to stay quiet. I like to be quiet when I rest and fill up in the presence of the Lord. I describe it as my intake valve. When I need to annihilate the enemy or call something forth, that's when everything I took in through being quiet comes out through audible prayer.
2. Pray and speak out in your native language. Spirit-filled Christians can become so comfortable praying in the spirit or tongues that it dominates their prayer lives. We must have a balance of praying in the spirit and praying in our native languages. If you find yourself

praying in tongues more than your native language, spend some time praying in your native language. Demons can't understand what you are praying in tongues; therefore, you must speak out, proclaim, and declare against evil forces when you encounter spiritual warfare.

3. Study the Book of Psalms and underline warfare prayers all in one color. Keep a highlighter by you when you study your Bible to underline scriptures that can be applied and prayed against spiritual warfare.

Spiritual Warfare Declarations

In Jesus' name I destroy every evil power and python spirit coming to suffocate my spiritual walk and prevent my prophetic destiny.

I annihilate every principality and power being sent forth to disrupt my prayer time. I bind and restrict all distractions. I say that my mind will stay focused.

I rebuke and renounce any witchcraft and Jezebel curses being released into the spiritual realm on my behalf to silence the voice of the prophetic and interrupt my prayer time. In Jesus' name I obstruct these curses from going forth.

I extinguish demonic forces that would go forth based on self-imposed word curses about facts I spoke out over my life that I was unaware had power and authority in the spiritual realm. I rebuke every word I have spoken that has been a detriment to my spiritual walk and prayer life.

When I speak, my words are prophetically assigned and targeted to hit the spiritual realm accurately. God sends forth His word and performs it over my life. My words have prophetic power and produce results.

Chapter 5

WALK IN DOMINION

EARLY IN MY Christian walk I picked up a book on dominion, and I devoured it in hours. I enjoyed learning the scriptures in Genesis about how God gave man dominion. I wanted that dominion! I took what I learned and ran with it. One of the most notable stories my husband still tells today is how, when our dishwasher motor started to make loud, weird noises, I would go and lay hands on the dishwasher and command it to quiet down and work properly. I had my office in the home, and I didn't need distractions. My money is God's money. I didn't want to spend kingdom money on a new dishwasher when I knew I could spend my money on something that would change people's lives and truly advance God's kingdom. No matter who was around or what I was doing, for three months I would get up when that motor would begin to grind, and I would command that dishwasher to work properly in Jesus' name. The results were that dishwasher lasted me eight more years.

I continued to learn about how Jesus gave us authority. But I didn't just learn; I applied it. It is one thing to know about something, but we have to implement it in our lives. Knowledge without application is just a brain full of information that we never allow to change us or those we influence. Taking my God-given authority over things and situations worked for me, and I want it to work for you too.

I don't believe exuding authority is a name-it-and-claim-it game. I believe we have authority over things, but we have to be in alignment with God's will and God's Word. The Spirit should quicken us as to what and when to take authority. He is our Guide, and we should depend on Him. We need to be tuned in to Him and His direction. Walking in authority is contingent upon having a personal close relationship with the Holy Spirit. We manifest our destiny and dominion when we rely on the Holy Spirit.

I have since taken authority over finances, healing for pets, deliverance from demons, book-writing contracts, favor with man, and much more! God has opened divine doors for me and bound and restricted the enemy from working against me because of authority I have exuded and words I have spoken audibly. I've said it before, and I'll say it again: your words are prophetically assigned and targeted to get results. When you speak, the spiritual realm must respond.

However, we need to know our authority and identity to have the confidence that our words are laced with Holy Spirit fire and power. We have the same power inside of us that raised Jesus Christ from the dead. We have resurrection life, power, and authority! We are citizens of heaven and have been given a kingdom inheritance to release here on earth. What will you release with the knowledge you have and the power you exude? The very Holy Spirit is inside you, and He is powerful and full of authority!

Prophetic Exercise: Release Authority

Declare out right now an audible prayer in short sentences of something you need to take authority over. Do you need something to change in a relationship, employment, finances, or health? Speak out and command your situation to turn around. You can look at the Prophetic Proclamations at the end of each chapter as a guide.

IDENTITY IN CHRIST

If someone asked you who you are, what would be your response? Do you identify as a parent, professional, or homemaker? Would you respond with, "I am kind, boisterous, or fun"? From time to time I hear people with disabilities use the words, "I am disabled." They identify with their disabilities and allow them to define who they are.

I once heard a pastor minister to a person having a conversation. The person said, "I am a divorcée." The pastor disciplined the person and said, "That is *not* who you are. Don't identify yourself that way."

People often identify themselves by past circumstances, current situations, failures, or accomplishments. Situations may have confronted you and circumstances may have manifested, but they are not your identity. Your profession, family role, and duties are not your identity either. You are not a doctor, pastor, author, janitor, or housekeeper. Ultimately you are a child of God and a citizen of heaven. This should be the first response that you release out of your mouth.

My response would be, "I am the daughter of the Most High King (Jesus Christ)." It is who I am, and kingdom citizenship and heavenly inheritance are my portion. I am valued, loved, chosen, and forgiven. I identify with the kingdom of God and who I am in that kingdom. Why? Because Romans 8:15 says, "For you have not received the spirit of slavery again to fear. But you have received the Spirit of adoption, by whom we cry, 'Abba, Father.'" I am adopted! My heavenly Father has created me and adopted me into His bloodline. Therefore I am a kingdom citizen.

There was a time when I wouldn't have answered this way. I struggled with fear for years. It was a generational curse, and I attempted to get free for years. When I felt as if it was a part of who I was, I would quote Romans 8:15. When fear wanted to creep in through a conversation or negative thought, I would have to talk myself out of it.

I did this by telling myself I was not the same person anymore. I wasn't a product of a generational curse that followed my bloodline. I was adopted by my heavenly Father and had the bloodline of Jesus Christ. This helped me to receive my identity. I had to transfer my identity from how I identified with my earthly parents to my heavenly parent. I had to change my mentality. When I didn't capture the thought, I didn't walk in my spiritual identity. Instead I walked in an identity of victimhood and defeat, feeling that I would never break free from the generational curse of fear.

The identity I knew was one of lack, fear, and other pessimistic thoughts. I took on fleshly thoughts instead of walking in the Spirit. I needed a mental transformation. "Do not be conformed to this world, but be transformed by the renewing of your mind, that you may prove what is the good and acceptable and perfect will of God" (Rom. 12:2). The Bible instructs us not to be conformed to this world. We cannot mold our identities into the world but instead need to have our kingdom citizenship mold us.

Your identity is in Christ, not in the circumstances. We can discover who we are in Christ by reading the Book of Galatians. "You are in Christ," my apostle would say. "You need to be one with the Word and the Word one with you." Jesus is the Word. Therefore we must be one with Jesus. When we are in Him and His Word, we will discover and live in our identities in Christ.

AUTHORITY

Jesus left this earth and gave us His authority. In the world, people are appointed to be another person's power of attorney. They are given the authority to make decisions on behalf of the person. They have authority over that person's bank accounts, medical decisions, life, and even death. Jesus gave us this kind of authority when He left earth and went to heaven. You could say Jesus gave us His power of attorney. He gave us the power and authority to heal disease, cast out demons, and raise the dead. "He called His twelve disciples to Him and gave them authority over unclean spirits, to cast them out, and to heal all kinds of sickness and all kinds of disease" (Matt. 10:1).

The *English World Dictionary* definition of *authority* is "the power or right to give commands, enforce obedience, take action, or make final decisions."[1] You have the right and power to give commands, take action, and make final decisions. You have the right to order the devil and evil spirits around instead of the devil ordering you around. You have the right to enforce obedience and order the spiritual realm to activate on your words. You can change your situation with the power of your words.

Jesus spoke audibly and took authority in the Gospels

over the fig tree, storms, food (bread and fish), sickness, and the demonic. He consistently modeled for us how to take authority. He spoke into the spiritual realm, and a natural result happened.

Our authority comes through the name of Jesus. "Therefore God highly exalted Him and gave Him the name which is above every name, that at the name of Jesus every knee should bow, of those in heaven and on earth and under the earth" (Phil. 2:9–10). When we ask by faith, in His name and according to the will of the Father, we will see the fruit of the authority we release. "I will do whatever you ask in My name, that the Father may be glorified in the Son" (John 14:13).

You have prophetic power in your words. You have the power to create, restrict, bind, loose, and call forth. When you speak according to the Holy Spirit's leading, the spiritual realm must respond to your words as you take authority over situations. The disciples and Jesus used their authority to heal the sick, raise the dead, and cast out demons. We, too, need to exercise our authority if we want to see battles subside and people's lives changed. We have the Spirit of God inside to lead and empower us. Now we need to learn our authority in Christ and then release it. Removing obstacles such as doubt and unbelief is critical in this process.

When you speak to a part of your body that needs healing, when you cast a demon out of your mind, and when you want to change your circumstances, do it in the name of Jesus. "How?" you may ask. Under the leading of the Holy Spirit, say whatever you command or decree followed by, "In the name of Jesus." Paul told us in Colossians 3:17, "And whatever you do in word or deed, do all in the name of the Lord

Jesus." Do it in the name of the Lord Jesus, our Messiah. In His name nothing is impossible, and everything is possible.

I have been in planes with storms and severe turbulence. I get on that plane, tap my hand to the side of the plane as I enter, and say, "I take authority over this plane to work properly and command no turbulence." One time we had the worst landing of my life. As we were landing on ice, we were skipping on the runway. People thought we were going to crash. The pilot didn't have control over the plane and couldn't stop. I got concerned and decided it was time to intervene. I declared audibly two times, "Plane, you will stop in Jesus' name." The plane stopped skipping, bouncing, jumping, and the pilot was able to get it under control.

Paul cast out a demon when he took his authority. "And this she did for many days. But Paul, greatly annoyed, turned and said to the spirit, 'I command you in the name of Jesus Christ to come out of her.' And he came out that very hour" (Acts 16:18, NKJV). Paul said, "I command." What could happen differently in your life if you commanded what you needed to happen?

Peter healed a man who couldn't walk. Not only could Jesus heal, but His power could heal people through His disciples. That same power heals today. When we believe in Jesus Christ and have been filled with the Holy Spirit, we have the healing power of Jesus living inside. "Peter said, 'Silver and gold I do not have, but what I do have I give you: In the name of Jesus Christ of Nazareth, rise up and walk'" (Acts 3:6, NKJV). Peter gave a simple command, "Rise up and walk," and a man who couldn't walk was healed. What if Christians went around with authority and faith, made simple commands, and believed in faith that they and others would receive what is being decreed into the spiritual atmosphere? How much different would our world be?

Reign in Dominion

Authority is good, but I want to make you reach for more and have you walk in dominion. I explain authority as something we release as we need it. We see a need, pray for the Holy Spirit's leading, and release our authority. As Christians it should not stop with authority; we should rule and reign in dominion. Let me explain dominion in a way that perhaps you can understand regarding another topic. When we worship, we may lift our hands and feel the presence of God, and it is good. There are times we go past the presence of God, and we feel the weightiness of His glory. It is as if holy fear comes upon us, and sometimes we think, "Oh my, God is right here, right now." In worship we can feel the energy or thickness of God's weighty glory in the atmosphere. God's glory manifests differently. However, we know God's glory is the ultimate place to achieve in worship.

With worship we move through the presence to get to the glory. With authority we move past authority to walk and rule and reign in dominion. Learning about our authority is good. We can heal sickness and disease, change our circumstances, and cast out demons. However, I believe many times after we have prayed with authority, we put that authority back on the shelf until we need it again. But dominion should be something we rule and reign in, not something we pick and choose when to use. It should be the very core and essence of our beings.

The Hebrew word for *dominion* is *radah* (raw-daw), which

means to tread down, subjugate, have dominion, prevail against, reign, or rule.[2]

> Then God blessed them, and God said to them, "Be fruitful and multiply; fill the earth and subdue it; have dominion over the fish of the sea, over the birds of the air, and over every living thing that moves on the earth."
>
> —GENESIS 1:28, NKJV

We have dominion over the earth, over everything. A spiritual shift needs to happen in our minds: when we see that we are in such a place of authority and dominion, we will rule and reign in it. It is ours! It is not a prideful thing to acknowledge. It is receiving the place of inheritance our Father created for us.

We read in Genesis 1:26, "Then God said, 'Let Us make man in Our image, according to Our likeness'" (NKJV). *Our* indicates the Trinity—the Father, Son, and Holy Ghost. We know that the Trinity has dominion and authority over everything. Therefore, since our identity is in Christ and we are made in the image of God, we have His dominion. The Holy Spirit is in us, God gave us dominion, and Jesus gave us His authority.

We have authority, and no harm can come to us if we exude that authority. The enemy may attack and try to penetrate us, but as we confess God's Word, we can be healed, delivered, and protected.

> I give you authority to trample on serpents and scorpions, and over all the power of the enemy. And nothing shall by any means hurt you.
>
> —LUKE 10:19

> These signs will accompany those who believe: In My name they will cast out demons; they will speak with new tongues; they will take up serpents; if they drink any deadly thing, it will not hurt them; they will lay hands on the sick, and they will recover.
>
> —Mark 16:17–18

Jesus said, "In My name they will cast out demons." The disciples used His name, and the spiritual powers that plagued people left. Those are the promises that God's Word gives us. We have the authority; we have been given dominion over all the earth and the devil and his demons, sickness, and disease. Now let's not only use our authority but walk in dominion over the earth as God intended.

It's Time for Activation

Use your God-given authority and your voice to walk in dominion.

Prayer of Repentance, Renunciation, and Breaking Agreement

I break agreement with and renounce passivity and complacency. I repent of not releasing my authority. I ask You, Holy Spirit, to convict me and help me be bold in my faith and release the authority Jesus gave me. Lord, teach me the truth of Your Scriptures. I speak and decree that I will use my authority to impact the world for Your kingdom. I will release my authority, prophetically led by the Holy Spirit. May releasing authority show people the glory of God and edify the name of Jesus.

Impartation and Activation Prayer

Jesus, thank You for giving us authority. Help me to use my authority. I believe when You died on the cross, You conquered the powers of darkness. Allow me to continue what You accomplished and heal the sick, cast out demons, and take authority over all things. I receive the Word of God and everything it says I can have. You have given me Your power of attorney to use here on earth. Holy Spirit, help me to release what has been entrusted to me. In Jesus' name, amen.

Prophetic Proclamations (Faith Declarations)

I have authority and dominion over all things on earth. I activate and release the authority I have been given.

I will rule and reign in dominion, which is the power to direct. I can direct the enemy to stay away from me instead of him directing warfare against me.

I will obey the Holy Spirit without delay as He quickens me to operate in the authority given to me. I will not be intimidated by what others think when I declare my authority audibly.

I pronounce that I have weaponry that is useful and effective against the kingdom of darkness. I have a voice, and I am going to use it with love and boldness.

I direct my words to hit a spiritual target with accuracy. When I speak, my words are prophetically assigned to hit a spiritual target and produce a natural effect.

Spiritual Activation

1. Write a ten-sentence declaration stating what you have to take authority over.
2. Read one book on authority and search out scriptures on authority.
3. Make a list of prayer requests that have been unanswered, and seek the Spirit's direction for a plan to take authority over those items.

Spiritual Warfare Declarations

I abolish every dark force that comes against my receiving supernatural biblical revelation. Deaf and dumb spirits, I bind and restrict you and command you to desist from your assignment.

I demolish every demonic deployment against my family. I command warfare attacks to cease in Jesus' name.

I paralyze every demonic assignment against me, and I command them to cease and desist of their activation of destruction against my prophetic destiny.

I command all financial embargos sent forth against my family and me to disperse in Jesus' name, and I proclaim that we have prosperity.

I cancel the assignment of all demonic entities called to send retribution. I speak and declare that the blessing and favor of God are upon me; therefore, in Jesus' name I abolish the plans of retribution and command such plans to break down, fall, and collapse.

Chapter 6

BUILD A WARRIOR'S HEART

BUILDING A WARRIOR'S heart takes effort. We need to develop two aspects of a warrior's heart. First of all, to create a warrior's heart, we have to root out offense, rejection, control, and pride from our lives. Second, we have to put in the time and know the value of being in the secret place and developing a deep relationship with the Holy Spirit.

I didn't always have a warrior's heart. I remember a season of being overemotional and crying when ministering in healing rooms. I thought, "How can I minister if I am constantly crying along with the person I am ministering to?" It is good to have compassion, but when we hear another person's story, and it frequently moves us to tears, there could be something in us that needs to be healed.

I've learned over the years that while we seek our deliverance and attempt to become spiritually strong, God will often put people in our paths who have "junk in their trunk" and need emotional healing in a certain area because this reveals to us what needs to be rooted out of us. Let me be more specific. If you are in denial that you have control issues, God might put controlling people in your path. It should be a spiritual checkpoint and self-evaluation stop for you when someone rubs you the wrong way or you see someone as an irritant in your life. Train yourself to use these encounters as a caution sign to check yourself.

I want to clarify that crying is not a sign of weakness. I know many people have been taught to stuff their tears. I encourage you to release your emotions when it is merited. However, being weepy every time I heard a sad story was a generational curse of being overemotional. After I received overwhelming love and healing from God, I needed my emotions to be balanced out. A warrior's heart is made of love, compassion, balance, and strength. If I didn't have a warrior's heart, I would experience offense, rejection, and turmoil due to the intransigence that comes with being a deliverance minister.

ROOT OUT STRONGHOLDS

Rooting out strongholds is crucial because we become vulnerable to emotional attack as we combat spiritual warfare and get involved in kingdom building. Jesus could have taken offense with the Pharisees, but He didn't. They were accusing Him of being demonic, which alone is an offense. He could have taken in rejection, but He kept His focus. We, too, must be like Jesus.

> Then one possessed with a demon was brought to Him, blind and mute, and He healed him, so that the blind and mute man both spoke and saw. All the people were amazed and said, "Is He not the Son of David?"
>
> But when the Pharisees heard it, they said, "This Man does not cast out demons, except by Beelzebub the ruler of the demons."
>
> Jesus knew their thoughts and said to them, "Every kingdom divided against itself is brought to desolation.

> And every city or house divided against itself will not stand. If Satan casts out Satan, he is divided against himself. Then how will his kingdom stand? And if I cast out demons by Beelzebub, by whom do your sons cast them out? Therefore, they shall be your judges. But if I cast out demons by the Spirit of God, then the kingdom of God has come upon you."
>
> —MATTHEW 12:22–28

A warrior must stay focused on the battle and not allow damage to his weaponry. When we allow rejection and offense to penetrate our armor, we aren't fully protected as we go to war. Build up your shield of faith and put on your helmet of deliverance to help protect your heart as warfare attacks try to infiltrate your armor. (See Ephesians 6:16–17; Proverbs 4:23.) Release unshakable faith and build a heart that will withstand assaults of the enemy and people. (See Psalm 62:3.)

Offense, rejection, control, and pride are still active in the church today and cause disunity. We are exploring how to release prophetic spiritual warfare, but we cannot effectively engage in battle if these ministry killers and destiny stealers have us in bondage. The detriment of these four strongholds, which I call blinding spirits, is that we don't know we are in bondage to them. People in bondage to them don't realize they are in bondage.

- Pride prevents us from seeing we are in bondage.
- Offense thinks everyone else is wrong.
- Rejection is a hidden stronghold.

- No one ever wants to admit they have control issues.

Therefore, instead of being released from these strongholds, we stay in bondage to them.

I was bound in pride and control for years. I did not see it. My husband would tell me. I knew I had a level of control and pride—everybody does—but I didn't realize how bad it was. Apostle Bernard Evans, who is my accountability as an overseer to my ministry, would tell me I had pride and control. I would continually deny it. One day I saw it. I was shocked by how blinding it was. I was even more shocked that I had never seen the bondage I carried, even though I was a deliverance minister who had helped thousands of other people. Looking back, I know God can use that experience. Even though I'm not glad I had pride, I'm thankful for the revelation of that experience on the blindsiding effect of pride. It helps me free other people who don't see they are in bondage. I can relate to them by telling them I experienced it too.

Pride was a stronghold for me. There are many strongholds by which we can be afflicted. In my book *Unshackled* I discuss the top ten strongholds. When engaging in spiritual warfare, there are four strongholds I strongly suggest you root out of your life.

Nullify and Identify Four Strongholds

1. Offense

The spirit of offense begins with unforgiveness after a person has been mistreated or hurt in a situation. The person gets upset and feels he or she is entitled to justification, retribution, or an apology. "'Vengeance is Mine. I will repay,' says the Lord" (Rom. 12:19). It is our responsibility to release forgiveness, not hold people accountable for their actions or desire penance. When an injustice occurs, the desire for reckoning begins to build a stronghold within our souls. Unforgiveness, when not released and walked through, leads to a strongman of offense. Once offense grows, the person begins to think everyone else is wrong and he or she is always right. Pride accompanies offense, forming a deadly duo of bondage that needs to be released.

2. Rejection

Rejection is a battle of the mind with lying and deceptive spirits. The person who suffers rejection is not lying or acting deceptive, but the spirits that attack that person's mind are lying and deceptive. Rejection is not uncovered at first because the people who suffer rejection try so hard to be people pleasers to gain acceptance. They don't realize their fear of rejection is driving their behavior. There can also be known rejection from family and friends, leaving a person to feel defeated and victimized. Rejection follows throughout a lifetime until people have deep deliverance and can conquer mind-binding spirits that lie to them and penetrate their thoughts.

3. Control

Issues with control are common. A controlling spirit usually manifests as a generational curse, mostly from our moms, but it can also manifest through our dads. Those who are dominated by a spirit of control can act in a variety of ways; therefore, it isn't always easy to identify. There are many root sources and entry points, such as never being in control, always being controlled, and being in an abusive relationship. Receiving deliverance from a controlling spirit is contingent upon the person wanting to give up control. Allow Him to bring you into brokenness, a place of complete surrender and dependence upon Him, and all control will be evicted.

4. Pride

Pride is sneaky and is multifaceted. Identifying pride in others is reasonably easy. I like to say people wear pride on their sleeves. Our own pride usually goes undiscovered until we've had a battle or confrontation with another person or the Spirit of the Lord begins to convict us of pride. I was not able to identify pride in myself because it manifested differently. The pride I experienced was not a blatant pride in my thoughts and actions. You may look at another person and say, "I don't have that characteristic or act that way; therefore, I don't have pride." We all need to ask the Holy Spirit to convict us and expose our hearts' intentions to see where pride manifests, because everyone does have a level of pride.

CONVICTION AND CORRECTION BRING DELIVERANCE

Allow the Holy Spirit to convict you and correct your actions, thoughts, and motives. Jesus tells us what will happen when the Holy Spirit arrives. "When He comes, He will convict the world of sin and of righteousness and of judgment" (John 16:8). It isn't easy to put ourselves out there and be vulnerable and humble, but something wonderful will come forth as we do. To be victorious in spiritual warfare requires a warrior's heart. The heart of a warrior cannot be made where strongholds exist. Therefore, a willing mind and heart are needed to allow the Holy Spirit to reveal those things in us; we don't want to be exposed or to have ignored or not realized there are issues. One of my life scriptures has been, "Create in me a clean heart, O God, and renew a right spirit within me" (Ps. 51:10). I also invite the Holy Spirit to "search me, O God, and know my heart; try me, and know my concerns, and see if there is any rebellious way in me, and lead me in the ancient way" (Ps. 139:23–24).

Spend time in the secret place, and get to know the Holy Spirit. He will lead you through deliverance. Allow Him to convict you and then obey what He speaks to you. It will lead you to healing and freedom.

Develop a Heart of Confidence

A warrior's heart is also confident. It is a heart on a mission to reveal the kingdom of God. It serves God and serves people; it loves God and loves people. Confidence comes when you realize what God has called you to do and who He has called you to be. You know He has called you to advance His kingdom. But are you poised in the anointing He has put upon your life?

Our assurance for the assignment comes not only from love but also from determination. When we accept that God has given us a prophetic duty to complete, being able to rest with that assignment will help us persevere to accomplish with all diligence what is set before us. If we are unworthy, insecure, or timid in our mission, we could waver instead of being full of strength as He gives us our marching orders, the direction He wants us to walk out and manifest here on the earth.

Evil spirits are committed to wreaking havoc on your life. They are devoted to releasing spiritual warfare attacks. You must be faithful to your objective to serve the Lord and people. Your heart must be rock solid, strong, and determined to complete your prophetic assignment. Warfare can wear you down. If you don't have a heart of love for God and His people, you will get weary and may give up on the way to your most significant victory. Elijah gave up after his victory. He killed all the false prophets with a sword, and now Jezebel was coming after him to kill him. Elijah ran for his life, and he prayed to die. (See 1 Kings 19.)

Abraham didn't give up when God called him to give up his son. Can you imagine God calling you to slaughter and sacrifice your only son? To say it would be tough is an understatement. But Abraham kept the vision. He kept the goal in mind. I'm sure his flesh was screaming, "No, Lord, don't make me do it!" But he was focused! Abraham feared God and served God wholeheartedly.

Don't give up on what the Lord has called you to do. You have been given a kingdom that cannot be shaken. (See Hebrews 12:28.) I like how the Complete Jewish Bible states it: "Therefore, since we have received an unshakeable Kingdom, let us have grace, through which we may offer service that will please God, with reverence and fear." Fearing God and offering service that pleases Him are attitudes of the heart. Have you identified the condition of your heart?

Diving deeper into Hebrews 12:28, we see the keywords and components such as *service*, *reverence*, and *fear*. The *American Dictionary of the English Language* gives us a good explanation that sums up these three words. *Reverence* means "fear mingled with respect and esteem; veneration."[1] *Veneration*, as defined by Webster's, is "respect or awe inspired by dignity, wisdom, dedication."[2] "The fear acceptable to God is a *filial* [Webster's defines it as "relating to, or befitting a son or daughter"[3]] fear, an awful [inspiring] *reverence* of the divine nature, proceeding from just esteem of his perfections, which produces in us an inclination to his service and an unwillingness to offend Him."[4]

Love Is a Weapon

Building a warrior's heart is creating a heart full of God's overwhelming love. Remove any hardness of heart, and allow God to fill your heart with His love. We put up self-protective walls and guard our hearts, but I believe some of us harden our hearts toward God and people in the process. Love is a weapon and a powerful one at that. The enemy cannot compete with a heart of love. Allow the heavenly Father to fill your heart with love. We need to receive love but also release love. Love must encompass every part of our beings and exude in all ways internally and externally.

Receiving the love of the Father isn't easy. Christians have two obstacles in accepting the love of the Father. The first one is unresolved sexual abuse issues. When a person has been sexually abused and has not received proper inner healing and deliverance from trauma or abuse, it is difficult to accept the love of Father God. The second one is earthly father issues. You may have difficulty connecting with the heavenly Father because your earthly father abandoned you, divorced your mom, sexually abused you, was unrelatable, or was a workaholic or alcoholic. The National Center for Fathering reports that only 3–4 percent of dads had fathers who said, "I love you," on a consistent basis.[5] When you don't hear your earthly father, who is here in a physical body, say,

"I love you," it is difficult to receive that your heavenly Father, whom you can't see, loves you.

Build a Heart of Love

Upon receiving healing, we need to build a heart full of love. I'd like to say it's natural that we get this overwhelming love inside us, but I've found in my years of ministry and personal experience that it doesn't always happen. How do you gain love? Ask for it! Our Father "is a rewarder of those who diligently seek Him" (Heb. 11:6).

I remember being in Missouri once for one of our prophetic ministry tours. As I was there to minister on the streets, the Lord called me one day to stay in my hotel room. I thought, "Really, Lord? You've brought me all this way to lock me up in a hotel room?" It was one of the most powerful encounters I've had as I lay on the hotel bed for an hour, speaking out, "I love You, Lord." I kept repeating those words and received the greatest love shower from the Lord. There have been additional times—whether driving, in worship, or walking—that I've asked the Lord to do this again so I can share His love with more of His people.

As I write this book, I am in another season of focusing on His love. When I have many responsibilities and deadlines, I can get caught up in busyness instead of exuding the overwhelming love of the Father to others. Also it can be a little intense when I take authority over evil spirits. Still, my prayer to the Father is that He would help me exude love even in times of intensity. I want the person being delivered through my ministry to feel love amid his or her deliverance. I want to be a person who loves at all times. I want to be known for the quantity and quality in which I love.

How about you? Do you desire to be known as someone who exudes the Father's love? Here are four ways to gather love in order to give it away.

Prophetic Exercise: Love Impartation

Stop and pray right now! Ask the Father to shower His love upon you. Ask Him to overfill you with His love so you can give it away. Pray and ask Him to let you love as Jesus does—unconditionally and full of mercy and grace.

> Heavenly Father, fill me with the abundance of Your love. I want to radically and honestly love people as Jesus would. Let my heart be full of pure intentions. Pour out Your love on me so in return I can pour out Your love on others. Let me feel the great love You have for me and break down any barriers I have to receiving that love. In Jesus' name, amen.

How to Gather Love

Scripture

The Word of God is one of the best ways you can gain a love impartation. Read the Scriptures and study the context; you will be assured that we serve a God of love. All Scripture is a representation of His love. The Bible is a big book of love! Our Father loves us so much that He penned these Scriptures through people inspired by the Spirit of God! My overseer says we should be one with the Word and the Word one with us. What does that mean? We should be in the Word and know the Word so much that it becomes us.

Worship

When we worship, we connect our spirits to His Spirit. Worship is a place we can be intertwined and connected with the Father, Son, and Holy Spirit. Love is the emotion we experience in worship as we "enter into His gates with thanksgiving, and into His courts with praise" (Ps. 100:4). We were created to worship Him. We minister to the Lord as we worship out of love.

Worship has been that place for me where I have connected steadfastly with the Lord. I have had so many encounters with Jesus and visions where I have experienced His great love. Worship is a private experience full of His love. Don't wait to worship publicly with your congregation; make it a part of your daily walk with the Lord.

Prayer

Our prayer lives reflect our love for Him. When we love someone, we spend time with that person, which is how we show we care. We can't be in a relationship with someone we don't communicate with consistently. We need to talk and pray several times a day. The Bible says Daniel kneeled "three times a day, and prayed, and gave thanks before his God" (Dan. 6:10). In Psalms it says, "Seven times a day I praise You" (Ps. 119:164). We should be in prayer regularly throughout the day.

Quiet meditation and rest

One of the essential ways you can connect to the Spirit of the Lord is to rest in His presence through silent meditation. The first time the Lord called me to get away on a solitude retreat with Him, I was unfamiliar with the idea and had uncomfortable thoughts such as: What will I do? Will I be able to connect? Will I be able to enter in the presence of God, locked alone for forty-eight hours? I feared I would not be able to spend that much time alone with the Lord. I was so concerned I would bolt out of the cottage and go shopping in a nearby town that I had my assistant drop me off so I didn't have a vehicle.

My fears were unfounded, and the time away with the Lord turned out to be terrific, even though I do confess I had my assistant pick me up a few hours early. I spent the first twenty-four hours in the constant presence of the Lord. I remember staring at a picture on the wall for the first three hours and receiving revelation upon revelation. He led me through the first twenty-four hours step by step, moment by moment. I now cherish the intimate times alone with the Lord on solitude retreats. I start to get cranky when I haven't had my quota of "God time." My husband will even prompt me gently, "Why don't you go and be with the Lord? I can tell you haven't had enough time."

Unoffendable in God's Presence

What one thing do people in the world have in common, regardless of race, religion, gender, or age? We all want to be loved. I believe we all can also give love. The question is, Can we give love as the Father gives? The Bible tells us, "The greatest of these is love" (1 Cor. 13:13), and "God is love" (1 John 4:8).

We are created to worship and called to love. The love that should come forth is an abundance of love straight from the Father's heart. It is a love that pours out from an extension of the love we have received from being in the presence of our Father. We cannot pour out what we do not have. I notice that when I haven't been in His presence, I do love, but I don't love abundantly. The presence of God is a place where we are saturated with His love, and we feel safe and protected. Our hearts should be so overflowing with His love that people can tell through the words we speak: "For of the abundance of the heart his mouth speaks" (Luke 6:45). If we don't speak and overflow love, we probably have not had enough time in the secret place.

God's presence isn't just about having enough love to pour out to others. It is also a place where we find safety and rest emotionally, physically, and spiritually. I like to say it this way: when we are in continual communion and fellowship with Him, nothing can touch us. Offense, anger, and controlling spirits from other people can try to attack us, but they roll right off because His presence is around us, and no unclean thing can exist in His presence.

Would you believe me if I told you it is possible never to feel rejected or offended again? I have lived for years without offense. You can't offend me. Now, I'm not saying I don't get hurt or upset, but it never manifests to the level of offense when I do. You can't offend me because I stay in the presence of God where offense doesn't exist. If I sense offense, I know it is one of two things: an emotional reaction of my flesh or a demonic spirit desiring to attack my soul. Either way, I have authority over those things. Therefore I can rebuke and destroy offense before it plants its seed of dissent.

PSALM 91

Scripture tells us that when we are in the secret place, we have protection and rest. I love to study Psalm 91 deeply because it has many prophetic layers and profound revelation.

Revelation leads to impartation. Let's dive into Psalm 91 and have this become application.

> He who dwells in the shelter of the Most High shall abide under the shadow of the Almighty.
>
> —Psalm 91:1

Dwell is a power-packed word defined as to possess a place, remain, settle, take up a homestead, and establish habitation.[6] The deepest meaning of the word *dwell* is to stay in that place. It means we need to enter that secret place continually, and when we go out of that secret place, we still need to keep ourselves in the presence of the Lord. When we walk out of our prayer closets physically, we need to keep our minds, wills, and emotions still in that prayer place. As we continually keep our souls in that habitation, we are in a permanent place of rest and protection, which is one reason I say it is possible never to be offended again.

The Complete Jewish Bible truly hits this point home: "You who live in the shelter of *'Elyon*, who spend your nights in the shadow of *Shaddai*..." (Ps. 91:1, CJB). *Abide* is another key word, and it means to stay permanently, continue, endure, tarry under defense protection.[7] To abide is to yield. *Abide* and *dwell* are linked to the importance of being in the secret place and staying in that place.

The Bible is full of conditions and results. If we do something, then God will fulfill His promises. In this case, when we abide and dwell, He will protect us. We discover His protection as we further dive into this psalm.

> I will say of the Lord, "He is my refuge and my fortress, my God in whom I trust." Surely He shall deliver

> you from the snare of the hunter and from the deadly pestilence.
>
> —PSALM 91:2–3

The Complete Jewish Bible brings out a further revelation: "Who say to *ADONAI*, 'My refuge! My fortress! My God, in whom I trust!'—he will rescue you from the trap of the hunter and from the plague of calamities."

The Lord builds a fortress of protection around us as we are in the secret place. He will rescue us from the plague of calamities. It doesn't mean that nothing will ever attack us. But if we are attacked, we will have internal peace. As we stay in the secret place, I believe the Lord will supernaturally spare us from spiritual attacks, but I also think when the attacks come forth, we will be in peace.

IT'S TIME FOR ACTIVATION

Seek the presence of the Lord, and you will find love, protection, and peace.

PRAYER OF REPENTANCE, RENUNCIATION, AND BREAKING AGREEMENT

Father God, I repent and ask for Your forgiveness where I have not exuded love. I know some of the lack of love I experience comes from self-hatred, guilt, condemnation, shame, and unworthiness. I release these emotions and strongholds from my life. In the name of Jesus I cast out offense, rejection, pride, and control. I renounce every place of hate, discord, insecurity, and hurt. I repent for not being a forgiving person and not pursuing love or being a vessel of Your love. In Jesus' name, amen.

Impartation and Activation Prayer

Lord Jesus, I ask You to encounter me in the secret place. I love You and desire to spend time with You. Help me to remove outside noise and distractions in my life. Help me to be diligent in seeking You, and when I am with You, help me to give You all of me. You deserve my full attention. You offer unconditional and instant forgiveness when I ask. Please help me to release that forgiveness toward others so that no emotional wounds enter my soul. I love You, Lord, and I want to draw closer to You. Holy Spirit, lead and guide me as I seek You in the secret place, and engulf me in Your presence. In Jesus' name, amen.

Prophetic Proclamations (Faith Declarations)

My heart overflows with the love of the Father and exudes His great love to everyone. I feel Jesus' love for people and release it to them through words and actions.

I am a forgiving person. I choose to release forgiveness and not take offense when others have hurt, betrayed, or rejected me.

I speak and decree that God is love, and since God is love, I am love.

I proclaim that I am diligent in seeking the Lord. My time in the secret place is filled with intense encounters with the Lord.

I command all distractions in my life to be removed. No hindrances will stop me from becoming quiet before the Lord.

SPIRITUAL ACTIVATION

1. Pray and seek the Lord for a radical love encounter with Him. Spend time in fasting and prayer, crying out to the Lord and expecting to receive more of His love.
2. Repent and seek healing for any offense, pride, rejection, and control. Ask the Holy Spirit to come in and correct and convict you. As you spend time seeking deliverance, trust that you will receive it.
3. Be committed, organized, and disciplined to remain in the presence of God and exude love. Make a plan of action.

SPIRITUAL WARFARE DECLARATIONS

I abort every demonic mission sent to interfere with my being a vessel of God's love. Every evil dissension sent to harbor hate, anger, and offense, I pronounce you null and void in Jesus' name.

In the name of Jesus I command all evil tormentors to abolish their orders against me.

I eradicate the enemy from my mind. I speak and decree that my heart and soul are set apart for constructive use for the kingdom of God.

I speak and decree that I release hurt and offense immediately. I leave no room for the enemy. I rebuke and renounce rejection and selfishness in the name of Jesus.

I demolish every principality and power coming against me. I proclaim that I go in the strength and power of the Holy Spirit and am filled with an abundance of His love in Jesus' name!

Chapter 7

DEMONIC OPERATIONS AND HIERARCHY

In case you don't know it by now, there is a real war between angels and demons and between light and darkness! We must know our opponent and how he operates. The church has shied away from discussing evil spirits and the havoc they can wreak. In football, coaches and teams study their opponents' plays in order to know their next move and reaction to a situation. We must do the same in prophetic spiritual warfare. We must know our opponent, the kingdom of darkness, and be on the offense against its strategies and tactics. It doesn't mean we need to get carried away in studying the dark side, but we must know we have a real adversary who is out to get us, and no one is immune to him.

Until the body of Christ realizes there is a hierarchy of demonic powers set out to destroy us, we will not live in the victory Jesus intended. It is time to bring spiritual warfare education and deliverance ministry to the forefront of the church so we can arm God's people and finally get them battle ready.

Demonic troops are organized, committed, and disciplined to carry out their assignments. Similar to military troops, they are obedient to complete their destructive orders and will go to any means to accomplish the enemy's plans against you. There are foot soldiers, commanders, and guards—some are visible, but many are invisible. Whether they are lower-ranking demons or strongman spirits, they have the same assignment: to come against God's plans for your life.

The devil and his foot soldiers are committed to their cause. We, too, need to be committed to conquer in the spirit realm and advance the kingdom. It means you ask the Holy Spirit for discernment and revelation as you familiarize yourself with demonic strategies and tactics. Walking out a life of obedience and discipline and relying on the Holy Spirit will assist us in being totally sold out and committed to our cause and will give us an upper hand against the enemy.

When it comes to Satan's realm, you need to understand his army's organization and structure. As I said, evil spirits—and I will even bring into this witches, warlords, and satanists—are committed to their cause. But remember, there is nothing to fear. Jesus won the battle, and there are twice as many good angels as fallen angels (demons). Jesus conquered the powers of darkness, and now we are to be an extension of what He accomplished.

We ultimately know how the war ends; we are victorious, even when the battles are difficult. What if we could empower the body of Christ to be as committed to Jesus and the kingdom of God as the people serving the devil? In that case, we could win this fight and convert those who serve Satan into those who serve Jesus. I've always said that satanists, witches, and warlocks desire the same things we do: love and power. And we can give them that love and power. (See 2 Timothy 1:7.)

There is a hierarchy in the satanic kingdom. Knowing our adversary comes with knowing the levels of forces we fight against. You mustn't go forth with arrogance or false confidence when fighting high-level demons that the Bible calls principalities and powers. I hear people going into regions, and they bind, restrict, and attempt to cast out the principalities and powers in that region and experience extreme warfare or become sick.

Let's make this clear! We don't go into regions and territories all radical for Jesus Christ and start trying to overrule and take authority over principalities and powers. Often people who do this don't have authority in the region or an anointing for deliverance ministry. They are reckless individuals with pride and arrogance who try to destroy something they have no business eliminating. Now you may be saying, well, Kathy, I can't entirely agree. We have dominion over these things. Yes, we have dominion when God says we have dominion and gives us a prophetic assignment to tackle these things. In spiritual warfare, specifically when praying over territories and regions, you need to co-labor with the local pastors and ministry leaders who have authority over the region in which they preside. When dealing with high-ranking demons, you can encounter severe warfare. If you tackle principalities from a region you don't have authority over, they will resist and not leave. When anointed individuals assigned by the Lord for this task work together with local leaders, warfare will minimize, authority will be released, and strongholds will cease.

Remember, being prophetically led by the Spirit of God means we take on the Holy Spirit's assignments, and we don't try and create our own. Not every city to conquer is yours. Not every power that sits on a bank is yours to overthrow. Not every enemy that arises is yours to attack. This might sound tough, but tough love brings us back down to where God needs us to be. It keeps us teachable and continually partnering with the Holy Spirit.

There is a formula for how principalities and powers (territorial and regional demons) need to be attacked. First and foremost, we need to have an assignment and directive from the Lord to go after these rulers. We need a battle plan from the Holy Spirit, a time of prayer and fasting, and most of all we need to do it when we are spiritually strong and ready for battle. There has to be a convergence between the local leaders and intercessors. Anyone from outside the area must be sent by the Holy Spirit as a deliverance minister, apostolic leader, or someone who has a breaker anointing upon his or her life. It takes a team to collectively come together and converge to see the high powers thrown out of a region. See *Territorial Spirits* by C. Peter Wagner for more information on this subject.

Ephesians 6:12

> For our fight is not against flesh and blood, but against principalities, against powers, against the rulers of the darkness of this world, and against spiritual forces of evil in the heavenly places.
>
> —Ephesians 6:12

Before I define the hierarchy of the demonic kingdom in Ephesians 6:12, I'd like to release freedom in your life. Recognizing that our fight is not against flesh and blood but against evil forces will assist you to freedom. In other words, your struggle is not against a human being, such as a relative, friend, coworker, boss, or neighbor; your fight is against an evil spirit. This is the way the Complete Jewish Bible renders this verse:

> For we are not struggling against human beings, but against the rulers, authorities and cosmic powers governing this darkness, against the spiritual forces of evil in the heavenly realm.
>
> —EPHESIANS 6:12, CJB

Some people are challenging to love. You might be in conflict with them. Perhaps you love them, but you don't like them very much. The Holy Spirit revealed to me years ago to love the person but dislike the evil spirit that operates through that person. When you learn to separate the person from the evil spirit he or she is bound with, you can begin to tolerate, accept, and love the person. You become more forgiving and less irritated or upset when the person offends or angers you. When we realize that our fight is not against flesh and blood, we can separate the part we don't like from the person we love and are in a relationship with. This insight has brought much tolerance and freedom in my life, and I hope this revelation brings you freedom.

Prophetic Exercise: Challenging Relationships

Is there a challenging person in your life? Can you extend grace and forgiveness? Speak out this prayer to release love and understand the spiritual realm. You can additionally ask the Holy Spirit to partner with you in prayer and give you additional words to pray for the situation.

> I love [insert person's name]. I dislike the demon spirit operating through him or her. I forgive [insert person's name]. Lord, help me to separate the person I love—that *You* love—from the demonic spirit operating through him or her. I pray that You would bless [insert person's

name] and soften his or her heart to receive Your love. Jesus, take out the hurt in his or her heart so [insert person's name] can give love, be love, and receive love. In Jesus' name, amen!

Demonic Hierarchy

I've compared demonic forces to military troops, so let's discuss the ranks listed in Ephesians 6:12.

- **Principalities:** These are the chief rulers and highest powers in rank and order in Satan's kingdom. They hold significant power and authority in the spiritual realm.
- **Powers:** These are second in command in Satan's kingdom. They execute the orders and carry out destruction from principalities.
- **Rulers of the darkness of this world:** These spirits oppose God's purposes in a submitted, disciplined, and ordered fashion. When these spirits are given assignments to carry out, massive destruction goes forth.
- **Spiritual wickedness in high places, or heavenly places:** These are the most common demons we will encounter. They are evil forces in the heavenlies, in the spiritual atmosphere that we are most likely to penetrate.

Satan organizes his demon spirits, gives them order and assignments, and sends them out to steal, kill, and destroy. We have been given the armor of God to combat such attacks.

> So take up every piece of war equipment God provides; so that when the evil day comes, you will be able to resist; and when the battle is won, you will still be standing. Therefore, stand! Have the belt of truth buckled around your waist, put on righteousness for a breastplate, and wear on your feet the readiness that comes from the Good News of shalom. Always carry the shield of trust, with which you will be able to extinguish all the flaming arrows of the Evil One. And take the helmet of deliverance; along with the sword given by the Spirit, that is, the Word of God; as you pray at all times, with all kinds of prayers and requests, in the Spirit, vigilantly and persistently, for all God's people.
>
> —Ephesians 6:13–18, cjb

When we put on and activate the armor of God, we will be victorious in every battle!

The Unseen Battle

In Daniel 10 we can see firsthand the war that rages in the spiritual realm.

> But then a hand touched me, which set me on my knees and on the palms of my hands. He said to me, "O Daniel, a man greatly beloved, understand the words that I speak to you, and stand upright, for I have been sent to you now." And when he had spoken this word to me, I stood trembling.
>
> Then he said to me, "Do not be afraid, Daniel. For from the first day that you set your heart to understand this and to humble yourself before your God, your words were heard, and I have come because of your words. But the prince of the kingdom of Persia

> withstood me for twenty-one days. So Michael, one of the chief princes, came to help me, for I had been left there with the kings of Persia."
>
> —Daniel 10:10–13

Daniel prayed and fasted for twenty-one days. From the life of Daniel, we know he was a man of God who prayed consistently. He was not afraid to show his faith and commitment to God. He was a man of prayer. We could say Daniel was a prayer warrior and very seasoned in prayer. Yet his prayers were held up from being answered. A spiritual war took place. Daniel couldn't see this war, and neither can we. We fight an unseen battle, and an invisible enemy targets every prayer request we send up.

How do you combat the forces of darkness that come against your prayers? It might seem counterintuitive, but your first line of defense is to pray on the offense. Don't wait until defensive measures need to be taken to combat warfare. Pray forcefully with authority to bind and restrict the attacks being sent forth against you.

But how do you practically pray against unseen warfare? Think about what is happening or has happened in the past, what you struggle with, or what you fear. Those are prime-time targets for the enemy to come after. Therefore you need to target things he can attack by praying on the offense. If you know you struggle with rejection in relationships, start speaking out blessing, healing, restoration, trust, acceptance, and every other thing you need to make sure rejection doesn't manifest. Come against judgment, criticism, gossip, and betrayal. Ask the Holy Spirit for tactical measures and strategic words to pray against the warfare the devil wants to send your way.

Believe that when you partner with the Holy Spirit, He will give you the words to pray out strategically. It is time to get past simple prayers such as, "Lord, bless me," or, "Cover my family and me with the blood of Christ." While these prayers are good, they can become passive and routine. Avoid praying out of legalism, which keeps you from going further in your prayer life. Instead press in to receive more as you cooperate with the Holy Spirit.

Satanic forces will maximize every chance they get to inhibit your prayers from going forth. They are vile and have no other agenda than to steal, kill, and destroy. (See John 10:10.) Even though spiritual forces can hold up your prayers, you still need to pray with expectation. Believe that your prayers will manifest.

I remember a woman who asked me for help with deliverance on multiple occasions. She would experience freedom through our sessions, but at home her torment would return. Finally, one day, she said, "I'm done. It's easier to live with my demons than it is to get deliverance."

We can feel a similar way about our prayer lives. We can be tempted to take the easier route and pray passive prayers instead of being aggressive. When we pray on the offense, we wage war. Our prayers are targeted to combat the devil and the fight he throws our way. If we pray mousy prayers, we will get caught in the trap the devil has set for us.

It's Time for Activation

It's time to resist the temptation to pray passive prayers and activate yourself to pray on the offense.

Prayer of Repentance, Renunciation, and Breaking Agreement

I repent for living a life not grounded in the Word of God. I come against every dry bone in my body, and I prophesy and speak commitment and discipline into my life. I renounce and break agreement with python spirits to steal, kill, and destroy my destiny. I come against every dark power that has attempted to operate against me. I speak and decree that I am forgiven, and I forgive myself for anything causing warfare in my life. In Jesus' name, amen!

Impartation and Activation Prayer

Holy Spirit, teach me when and how to put on the armor of God. I thank You that You have provided stellar tools for me to conquer powers and principalities. I receive these tools and will dedicate myself to using them. Help me to be in Your Word and to put on truth. Help me to walk in shalom and be prepared for what You have. In Jesus' name, amen!

Prophetic Proclamations (Faith Declarations)

I proclaim I have strong weapons and artillery to use against the kingdom of darkness.

I will walk by faith and use prayer, Bible study, and worship as tools against the enemy.

I have every good and perfect thing I need to come against warfare attacks. The Holy Spirit is on my side and is my partner and friend.

I shall not fear when confronted with the powers of darkness, because Jesus is the light.

No weapon formed against me will prosper. My prayers will disperse every demonic arrow.

Spiritual Activation

1. Develop a prayer plan. You may think you don't need a plan, but if you aren't praying regularly, set alarms in your phone or figure out a way to be disciplined in your prayer time.
2. Pray and discern over your community. Strongmen usually sit on banking institutions and city halls. Go downtown in your region and pray and try to discern which principalities and powers are over your region. This exercise is to give you an opportunity to partner with the Holy Spirit to receive revelation. This is not a time for you to try and tackle and tear down the principalities. Open your spiritual ears and eyes and try to receive from the Holy Spirit.
3. Remember, the demonic realm is organized, disciplined, and committed. Ask the Holy Spirit to convict you of time stealers and destiny wasters. Where and how can you

get organized, disciplined, and committed to advancing the kingdom, increasing your prayer life, working through your deliverance, and manifesting your healing?

Spiritual Warfare Declarations

In the name of Jesus I dissolve every demonic attack against my marriage, children, and family, and I constrict the movement of every demonic spirit sent to cause disunity.

I bind and restrict evil forces from attacking my home. I speak a hedge of protection around my home that no weapon formed against it will prosper.

I rebuke the devourer and the plans he orchestrates against us. I say be exposed and may every dark plan come into the light. May my prayer be a weapon to strategically go against every destructive plan.

I paralyze the powers of darkness in my life and over the jurisdiction and sphere of influence Jesus has given me.

I restrict the enemy's movement in my life, family, and household in Jesus' name. I bind and restrict principalities from operating against us.

Chapter 8

EXPOSING DEMONIC INFILTRATION OF THE SOUL

We are three-part beings. Each of us has a soul (mind, will, and emotions), a physical body, and a spirit. We are spirit beings in flesh suits. When you've had a taste of God's goodness from being in His presence, it is uncomfortable to be in the flesh.

The closer I get to the Lord, the less I like my flesh. I don't like being emotional, getting upset, or even sometimes feeling. I want to be invincible! I don't want offense, rejection, or disappointment to penetrate me! I desire to be love, give love, and receive love without constraints. I wish I could say I am entirely spirit being, but that would not be true. Still, it is my desire to walk in the Spirit at all times.

Oppression vs. Possession

Before we delve into the topic of this chapter, I'd like to dispel the misconception that a Christian cannot have a demon. As Christians, demons can infiltrate our souls or our physical bodies, but they cannot occupy our spirits where the Holy Spirit resides. To break this down further: a demon can enter a believer's soul, which is the mind, will, and emotions, and it can take up residence in a believer's physical body.

An evil spirit can occupy a part of a believer's soul, but it cannot enter his or her spirit. We get hung up on the word *possessed*, which means to occupy. A demon can possess or occupy your soul but not your spirit. To be clear, a Christian can be demonically *oppressed* but not *possessed* in his or her spirit. However, a Christian can be possessed (occupied) but not fully taken over by a demon in his or her body or soul (mind, will, and emotions).

It's pretty straightforward: if a spirit of infirmity causes cancer, then it possesses that part of your body where cancer attacks. If a luring spirit possesses your mind and draws you into fear and depression, then it possesses part of your mind, but it does not possess your spirit.

When we study the Scriptures, we find that deliverance is for believers. Paul was talking to believers when he said, "Therefore submit yourselves to God. Resist the devil, and he will flee from you" (Jas. 4:7). We also know if we don't fill ourselves up with the Holy Spirit, demons will come back seven times worse. (See Matthew 12:45.) Again, this indicates deliverance is for believers.

A person without Jesus on the inside can be possessed by a demon controlling his or her actions. But a Christian who has surrendered his or her life to the Lord will only feel oppression, such as a strong luring spirit drawing them into natural or emotional sin. It will feel as if an invisible force leads you in the wrong direction, but it cannot possess your spirit.

When looking at our souls, we have emotional ailments that, when left unhealed, can develop into spiritual strongholds. One way demons can occupy your soul is when strongholds are not addressed during inner healing. Emotional ailments come because of stress or trauma. The ministry of inner healing prevents these from becoming demonic strongholds. When we fail to heal the trauma, it escalates, and then deliverance ministry is needed for a demonic spirit to be cast out.

Our physical bodies can be attacked with sickness or disease through trauma, accidents, generational curses, unresolved emotional ailments, not eating the right foods, being exposed to toxins, and several other circumstances. These can allow an open door for the enemy to come in and plague your physical body with a demon that manifests sickness and disease. People don't always experience physical healing when prayed for because a demonic spirit could be the driving force of that illness. A demon cannot occupy a Christian's entire body; that would be considered possession. However, a demon can occupy a portion of the body through physical sickness and disease, such as cancer.

We don't have to be afraid of this reality. Remember, "For our fight is not against flesh and blood, but against principalities, against powers, against the rulers of the darkness of this world, and against spiritual forces of evil in the heavenly places" (Eph. 6:12). We don't wrestle against flesh and blood but against principalities, powers, rulers, and spiritual forces, which are all demonic spirits.

Let's discuss the ways they find entrance into people's lives.

Entry Points

Demonic spirits can come into our physical bodies through generational curses, accidents, soul ties, near-death experiences, trauma, addictions, and sin. Eradicating these spirits at the entry points is essential. Entry points are exposed as we discern and quickly look back at our pasts to discover where evil spirits gained access. We can consciously open the door through sin. But we can also subconsciously allow an attack by not seeking our healing or being a target of the enemy because of God's call on our lives. Either way, the open portals of our souls need to be addressed.

Jesus conquered death at the cross, but how can we, as Christians, shut the door to spiritual attacks? Scripture tells us that when evil spirits depart, they can come back in if we don't close the doors to sin in our lives and passionately pursue a relationship with Jesus.

> When an unclean spirit goes out of a man, it goes through dry places seeking rest. Finding none, it says, "I will return to my house, from which I came." When it comes, it finds it swept and furnished. Then it goes and brings seven other spirits more wicked than itself, and they enter and dwell there. And the last state of that man is worse than the first.
>
> —LUKE 11:24–26

As we close demonic doorways, it is imperative to seek Him and His Word and to pray. I have seen the demons come back worse, just as Luke's Gospel says. The area where I see it the most is in average Christian believers. When they receive deliverance but aren't consistent in their pursuit of holiness and the things of God, that's when the demons return. This is multiplied in people who struggle with victimhood, defeat, and passivity.

Six Ways Demons Can Infiltrate the Soul

1. Trials and testing

Being continually attacked by the demonic realm can wear you down and wear you out. Suffering from repeated cycles of spiritual attacks can plague your mind and leave you feeling defeated. During times of trial, we need to make sure we humble ourselves before the Lord in prayer. Defeat and victim mentality can enter when we have been worn and beaten down. What we do during the trial and on the other side of it will have lasting fruit. "My brothers, count it all joy when you fall into diverse temptations, knowing that the trying of your faith develops patience. But let patience perfect its work, that you may be perfect and complete, lacking nothing" (Jas. 1:2–4).

We all face trials and tests, and we must embrace them. Embracing them doesn't mean we say, "Oh, goody! Look what is happening to me." It means we stop resisting them. Don't go against the grain; go with the grain. After we recognize and acknowledge we are being confronted with something in spiritual warfare, we will move through it easier if we stop fighting and embrace it.

2. Deception

Seducing spirits are luring spirits that draw you away from proper teaching and lead you into deception. We cannot assume that just because a teaching sounds good, it is accurate. People interpret scriptures in different ways. If you have a check in your spirit, are uncomfortable, or kind of shake your head at the teaching, then it very well could be the Holy Spirit giving you warning it is not accurate.

In 1 Timothy 4:1 the Bible says, "Some will depart from the faith and pay attention to seducing spirits and doctrines of devils." We must protect our souls and spirits the best we can. Most false teachers don't start out being untruthful; I think a good portion begin as good teachers but veer off along the way.

I recently bought a few books written by a well-known author. Some of the people who follow my ministry began using a practice he taught, and I wanted to understand more about it. I began to read these books and was unsettled. I took these books and went and searched Scripture to test this teaching. I went through the chapters and looked up the Scripture verses the book referenced to see if I could gain knowledge from the Scriptures to agree with what he was teaching. I was unsettled and could not receive the same revelation. I asked my husband to read some points of the book, and he also didn't see where Scripture aligned and was unsettled. I then called up one of my apostolic friends who knows a lot on the subject. I conveyed my feelings to him and asked him whether I was missing something. My friend said, "Kathy, you are answering your own question." I had a check in my spirit, and I needed to listen to it.

When receiving new revelation from the Scriptures, sit and meditate on it for a few minutes. Allow the Holy Spirit to come in and be your teacher. Deception comes from taking things at face value. I love to question God. When I receive an answer to prayer or discernment, I don't just take it in; I ask why. Testing everything is good!

3. Thought penetration

The devil is a liar. He is the father of lies. (See John 8:44.) We've all had negative thoughts in our minds. When an evil spirit is in your soul, it can attack your mind with negativity and lure you into wrong ways of thinking.

We connect our spirits to the Holy Spirit. We connect our souls (mind, will, and emotions) to the Father, Son, and Holy Spirit. Similarly, demons are spirit beings that infiltrate our thoughts. People who practice witchcraft do not always hear an audible evil voice, but they connect their souls to a demonic spirit. When a demon oppresses us, we can hear thoughts such as, "You will never get free," "You are no good," or "Why don't you go and kill yourself?" Demons are evil spirits in our souls, and they can penetrate our minds.

When witches and warlocks communicate with demons, they give their souls over to a demonic being. When we don't seek deliverance and have come into agreement with strongholds or have been victims of trauma, the same thing can happen: we can give a part of our souls over to the enemy. It is not the same as when a warlord consciously decides to unite with a spirit being. Still, by our lack of knowledge and slothfulness against deliverance, we come into unity on a lower level with a demonic entity. What we don't cast out, we enable and give access to part of our souls.

Society scoffs at the notion that when a person hears voices, those voices could be demonic. Instead they think the person has a mental illness, such as schizophrenia, and they want to resolve the problem only through therapy and medicine. It has been my experience that in the majority of cases, tormenting voices are demonic spirits. The ministry of deliverance must be brought forth if we want to set people free from their mental torment. Jesus cast out the demon and dealt with the root issue. He addressed it for what it was: a demon!

Demons love to torment people who struggle with mental issues. Therefore, regardless of the root cause, the approach remains the same. We have authority through the Holy Spirit and the shed blood of Christ to halt and expel any demons exploiting a person who is struggling mentally. I have met many mature, Spirit-filled Christians who have a history of mental illness or have children who do. They will often say that they have prayed and warred over their children, taken them through deliverance, anointed them with oil, renounced generational curses, and still the mental illness persists. Indeed, the roots and causes of mental illness and demonic oppression are complex, but know this: God *does* want to deliver you and your children!

The root cause might not be known (other than that we live in a flawed, fallen world full of disease and death). However, the spiritual dimension cannot and should not be ignored! Continue to pray against demonic influence. Whatever the problem, know that you serve a loving God who sees your pain, and the Holy Spirit is your Comforter and Deliverer. Realize that you have an enemy, and the forces of hell will indeed try to take advantage of your human weaknesses and ailments. Keep praying in faith; keep binding the enemy in order to remove any advantage.

4. Vain imaginations

Our minds are creative. I am always astonished when I watch *Star Wars* movies. I think, "How do people think these things up?" I am impressed with the unique characters and their appearances and ways of acting.

Did you ever wonder how vain imaginations negatively fill your thought life? Vain imaginations and false scenarios enter our minds. The truth is we put them there, and we entertain such thoughts by not dismissing them. We think and visualize things that will never happen. Strongholds are in our minds. By taking every thought captive and making it submit to the Word of God, we can clear our minds of negativity and doubt and live in the faith and belief that the Bible states. In 2 Corinthians 10:4–5 it says, "For the weapons of our warfare are not carnal, but mighty through God to the pulling down of strongholds, casting down imaginations and every high thing that exalts itself against the knowledge of God, bringing every thought into captivity to the obedience of Christ."

As we root out the strongholds in our minds, we gain a clearer understanding of how the lies and fear operate. Thoughts that enter our minds can be our flesh, vain imaginations, or demonic attacks. When we rerun thoughts in our mind and vain imaginations begin to manifest, it becomes difficult to decipher what is true versus false. Behind a stronghold or vain imagination is a lie, behind the lie is fear, and behind the fear is an area where we don't trust the Lord. When you discover the lie and recognize the fear, you can take every thought captive and cast out what is not of God.

5. Sin

Ephesians 4:27 says, "Do not give place to the devil." How do we give place to the devil? He gains access when we open the door by sinning. Closing the door must be our first step as we dedicate our lives to Christ. Sin can be something we consciously do, such as pornography, stealing, or lying; it can also be subconscious, such as being controlling, irritable, or angry. It can be a conscious act that we know we need to repent of or emotional behavior that we subconsciously don't realize has opened the door to the enemy. Inner healing and deliverance are important because they close the door and deny enemy access.

Disobedience can be in any area of your life: neglecting personal time with God, poor eating habits, out-of-control finances, and so on. If He tells you not to eat something or wants you to give up something, you need to be obedient.

Anytime you don't carry out His instructions, you are in disobedience to the Lord.

Prevent spiritual attacks by walking in obedience to the Lord's instructions. Live in alignment with Scripture. Be disciplined to carry out the orders and instructions He gives you.

6. Generational curses

Generational curses and learned behavior patterns are entry and access points to the demonic. The Bible tells us how curses pass through generations. "...keeping mercy for thousands, forgiving iniquity and transgression and sin, but who will by no means clear the guilty, visiting the iniquity of fathers on the children and on the children's children, to the third and the fourth generation" (Exod. 34:7).

These curses continue to build strongholds in our lives because many Christians feel as if Jesus took all our curses at the cross, and we no longer struggle with them. While Jesus did take our afflictions at the cross, we now have to walk out our salvation and deliverance. When you accepted Christ, did you automatically break free from your parent's high blood pressure, diabetes, or glaucoma? Have none of their physical ailments ever plagued your body? If you are free from the curse, you should not be on the medications your parents are on, or you should not be at high risk for generational illnesses.

Emotional ailments additionally run through our generational lines, such as depression, bipolar disorder, anger, control, and fear. Generally speaking, we are a product of how we were raised. I am not proclaiming that over your life negatively; I am stating that during our formative years, the behaviors modeled for us, the things we observed, and the way we were treated have a significant impact on who we become. These emotional ailments can be a generational curse, and since we have been given a new bloodline through Christ, we can break the curse and move out of personal affliction to victory.

RECEIVE DELIVERANCE FROM GENERATIONAL CURSES

We diagram a family tree to discover our family lineage. We write down our relatives' names and how they were related to us, and if we dig deeper, we usually find where they came from. Our family trees can contain information that is valuable to our spiritual walks and deliverance. Diagramming a family tree can help discover health ailments, emotional issues, and spiritual generational curses.

Prophetic Exercise: Generational Family Tree

How can you take what you know about your family line to bring about your physical healing and deliverance from emotional strongholds? When I lead people through generational curses, it isn't as easy as saying, "All generational curses be gone in Jesus' name." Evaluate and diagram your family tree of emotional and physical ailments. Create it just as you would a genealogical family tree with Grandma and Grandpa at the top, followed by your mom, dad, aunts, uncles, brothers, and sisters. You can even add your children to find out what is already being passed on to them.

As a guideline for what to diagram, look for negative circumstances they suffered that you are experiencing, such as:

- trauma

- poverty
- abortion
- divorce

Record any physical afflictions they have suffered, such as:

- near-death experience
- attempted suicide
- high cholesterol
- diabetes

Now list any emotional ailments they suffer, such as:

- depression
- anger
- bitterness
- fear

Write down as many things as you can under each person's name. Go through your tree and discover what repeats through the generations. What commonalities can you identify?

Prophetic Exercise: Break Agreement With Curses

Pray and ask the Holy Spirit where to start and to lead you through the healing process.

I want to stress the importance of speaking out loud the following guidelines. The demonic realm cannot hear what you pray in your mind. These things need to be spoken out into the spiritual atmosphere. Learn more about the importance of praying audibly in my book *SPEAK OUT.* (See the appendix.)

- Repent for your generations.

Say, "I repent for the sins of my grandparents, parents, and those before me. Lord, I ask for Your forgiveness on their behalf. I call off any assignments this has put on me and my generation."

- Repent for your actions and inactions.

  Speak, "Father, please forgive me for behavior patterns, habits, and addictions I took upon myself. Forgive me for what I knew and didn't know and for what I didn't try to stop and change."

- Break agreement.

  Proclaim, "I break agreement with the demonic spirits of generational curses. I call off any ill effect they have on me. I command that I will not co-labor with these spirits anymore. I decree and declare I have broken their legal right to take action against me."

Prophetic Exercise: Prayer of Victory and Thanks for Emotional Healing

When you are free of your emotional ailment, make it a practice to speak out and declare your victory. Declare the truth you know and a scripture that correlates to your situation.

> I thank You, Lord, that I am free from fear and that Your Word says, "For God has not given us the spirit of fear, but of power, and love, and self-control" (2 Tim. 1:7).

Prophetic Exercise: Physical Healing From Curses

Manifest your physical healing by calling forth and declaring healing into your body!

I break agreement with sickness and disease in my body and declare by His stripes I am healed (Isa. 53:5).

I command every generational curse of sickness [list the disease by name] to get out of me in Jesus' name.

I repent and renounce everything I participated in to enhance or co-labor with this disease [such as hang on to stress instead of releasing it] in Jesus' name. Spirit of stress, I command you to leave my body in Jesus' name.

I declare and decree, "I am redeemed of the curse."

Body, I speak to you and command you to line up with the Word of God in Jesus' name.

Health and healing are mine because of what Jesus did for me.

Soul Ties

Soul ties are demonic spirits that we inherit from people we are in a relationship with, including relatives, friends, coworkers, and ministry leaders. Soul ties infiltrate our souls when we spend time around people who are impure, emotionally unhealthy, or in need of deliverance from evil spirits. Soul ties can inflict us as we covet, idolize, or begin to have lustful feelings toward a person. A soul tie is a demon inherited from a relationship with another person. It is a place where another person can need inner healing and deliverance.

You can easily identify a soul tie when a new challenge or issue arises. Ask yourself whether your reaction is out of character for you. Are you behaving in a way that is unlike you? The next step is to see whether you can identify that behavior in a friend, relationship, or relative. Is there someone you have hung around with that you can see manifests this behavior or demon? Have you noticed you picked up the habit or characteristic? This could be a soul tie—a place in your soul that opened up to demonic influence. The soul tie has penetrated your mind, will, and emotions and has become a spiritual stronghold.

Soul ties also come from sexual relations. Suppose you are in a sexual relationship, which God considers a covenant. That sexual partner's generational curses can transfer to you. Therefore, keeping ourselves pure outside marriage is important, along with cleansing ourselves from all former relations. This is also why it's important to include any past or present sexual relationships through incest when you map out your family tree.

Let me share two pertinent examples. I was delivering an entire family of generational curses. We went back through five generations and diagrammed freak accidents, suicide, intellectual disability, and alcohol. As I worked with the family and wrote down the physical and emotional ailments, we began to see the curses' manifestations in marriages and unmarried sexual relations. It wasn't with one person but several people in the family line. The generational curses transferred over to soul ties and began to manifest themselves in nonfamily members.

Another case I remember was a couple who were high school sweethearts but married later in life. One of the person's parents had a rare, incurable disease. They got married, and within six months of the parent dying from the disease, the spouse contracted the disease and died. This shows how a soul tie can allow a curse to jump from one family line to another.

Delivering people from soul ties is not as simple as saying, "All soul ties be gone in Jesus' name." Sexual covenants must be broken and demonic strongholds evicted. Repent from and renounce emotional or sexual attraction and break agreement with any foothold to the demonic realm.

Generational curses and soul ties can be intertwined. When receiving deliverance from generational curses and soul ties, we must cast them out both collectively and separately. There is much more to this topic than I have room to share, but allow me to briefly explain, using rejection as an example. When we have a soul tie of rejection and a generational curse of rejection, it also opens a doorway for our own rejection and a familiar spirit of rejection. This is the same with any spiritual stronghold. Therefore, when evicting the spirit, we must address the generational curse and soul tie collectively, saying, "Generational curse and soul tie of rejection, get out in Jesus' name."

However, we also want to address them separately because in some cases the stronghold can come from a different person, whether in the case of a soul tie or a generational curse. When we call them out separately, we make sure we are covering all of our bases. In this case we would also need to cast out rejection, because when it becomes a generational curse, it is something we also take in and allow to take root. Additionally we would want to cast out a familiar spirit of rejection from repeatedly attacking us. When we break generational lines of curses, emotional ailments, sickness, and disease, we become bloodline breakers and blessing makers!

IT'S TIME FOR ACTIVATION

Pray this prayer audibly to break all curses being passed through your bloodline as well as any soul ties. Yield at the end of the prayer, and wait for the Holy Spirit to partner with you and give you discernment of what else needs to be prayed forth.

PRAYER OF REPENTANCE, RENUNCIATION, AND BREAKING AGREEMENT

I break agreement with every generational curse from my bloodline. All curses from the grave and past generations, I bind, rebuke, and cancel your effect on my health, emotions, and bloodline. I speak and decree that I am redeemed from the curse and that no sickness or plague will come near my dwelling. Every generational activation in the spiritual realm, I take authority over you now and call you null and void, totally canceled of every effect by the blood of the Lamb. I speak and decree that all known and unknown curses are broken off me, and any associated demonic spirits are cast out and evicted now in Jesus' name!

IMPARTATION AND ACTIVATION PRAYER

I thank You, Father, that I am a bloodline breaker and blessing maker. Your Word says cursed is he that hangs on a tree. I thank You, Lord, that You took the curse so I could be free. I receive my freedom in fullness! Lord, help me to become a blessing maker in my bloodline. Holy Spirit, convict me to guard my words so that I do not put curses on my children. I step out in faith and the strength of the Lord that old things have passed and all things have become new. I receive the new life You have for me—one of power, abundance, and joy. In Jesus' name. amen!

Prophetic Proclamations (Faith Declarations)

I proclaim I am a curse breaker and blessing maker. My bloodline is the bloodline of Jesus, free from curses, sickness, and disease.

I speak and decree that my faith is strong. My mind focuses on the truth of what God's Word says about me.

I repent of any curses I may have put on my children with my words and actions. I declare they are set free from my generational curses.

I proclaim that my eyes are fixed on Jesus. I do not put false idols, time stealers, and destiny wasters ahead of the Lord.

I believe and trust in the Word of God. I take what the Word says and believe it will be established permanently in my life.

Spiritual Activation

1. Discipline your mind. The battle is in the mind. Teach and practice a technique to

capture every thought as the devil attempts to permeate your mind.

2. Break generational curses. Go through this chapter, make the generational tree, and walk out your freedom from generational curses. If you need further assistance or want to learn more about breaking and severing generational curses, enroll in my e-course on generational curses. (See the appendix.)
3. Break soul ties. Keep yourself pure, and make sure you don't idolize or draw particularly close to anyone outside marriage. Seek the Holy Spirit for discernment, wisdom, and direction in relationships when a new person comes into your life whom you feel drawn toward or especially like. Take a step back and discern and inquire of the Holy Spirit about this person. Have the Spirit lead and guide you on how to proceed and how to establish safe boundaries. Allow the Holy Spirit to convict you if you should not move forward in a relationship with the person.

SPIRITUAL WARFARE DECLARATIONS

I bind and nullify every curse operating from my grandfather's grave. I cancel and obliterate in the spirit realm every vow, oath, dedication, and promise made on my behalf by Freemasonry curses from my grandfather's side.

I burn up in the spiritual atmosphere any ungodly soul

ties another person may have toward me. I speak and decree that there are no spiritual or soulish covenants by unclean or idolizing feelings. In the name of Jesus I cancel any spiritual darkness and curses put against my life.

I rebuke and take full authority over my thoughts. I do not give my thoughts space to run rampant with vain imaginations.

I repent of any sin and open doors I have activated. I remove legal rights and places where I took in generational curses and allowed them to operate in my life.

The enemy will not deceive me. I bind and restrict the enemy from plaguing my thoughts with lies. I rely on the Holy Spirit for prophetic insights.

Chapter 9

CONQUER EVERY THOUGHT

THE SAYING THAT the battle is in the mind couldn't be truer. I have fought those battles, and they aren't fun. One of the entry points to my mind was experiencing trauma through health ailments in my immediate family. As I mentioned earlier, our son, Dillon, had to be resuscitated twice at birth. Our daughter Amber almost died due to a medication allergy. My husband, Ron, was sent home from a hospital when X-rays were misread, and his appendix burst overnight. The trauma included my son going to the hospital for freak accidents the first twelve years of his life. Until we discovered a curse was at work, our daughter spent the first year of her life in and out of the hospital, and I woke up on a surgery table. I could have filed numerous malpractice suits for several different reasons, but suing is against my biblical convictions. Nevertheless, several medical circumstances we encountered left me fearing medical ailments. I also was surrounded by people who thought the worst when medical afflictions happened.

In the process of my deliverance, I had to list out every happening because the enemy would torment my mind when anything happened with my health. I even remember being a Spirit-filled preacher on the way to one of my events when seven different health symptoms manifested in my body two hours before I was to preach. Suddenly, as I was getting ready, all these things started to happen in my body to make me not feel good and make me fear something was wrong. I knew it was a demonic attack trying to torment me before ministering. I pressed through despite the torment, but that is how to describe it—torment. The enemy locks your mind down. You feel emotionally and spiritually paralyzed, unable to war and counterattack the agony. It is a mind-binding spirit that keeps you focused on the very thing you fear.

Capturing every thought and recognizing the lie is the key to your freedom. Even though the devil still tries to lure me into the fear of medical ailments, I can now recognize it is a demonic attack. Yes, occasionally I may have an actual symptom. Still, the devil would intensify the manifestation in my body by attacking me with a luring, mind-binding spirit to draw me into focusing on it and coming up with vain imaginations and false scenarios. I can now pray my way through and conquer medical conditions in my family, such as kidney stones, broken bones, medication allergies, and others, without physician intervention.

Luring spirits that draw you into focusing on the negative and the very thing you are trying to get free from won't permanently leave you alone. The devil wants to keep you in bondage. However, as we are empowered and recognize his attacks, we can rise above our situation and pray effectively against the kingdom of darkness. My daughter Lauren used to fight rejection. She would allow it to pierce her emotions for a few days or weeks at a time. I remember her coming into our living room, sitting down in my deliverance chair, and speaking out how she now recognized the lie. It brought her so much freedom to acknowledge the lie. When you realize the lie, you can dismiss it.

The Battle for Your Mind

The battlefield of spiritual warfare is in the mind. The enemy will penetrate your thoughts. Your soul (mind, will, and emotions), which is the fleshly side of you, will arise with vain imaginations and false scenarios. Recognizing his lies will put you on a pathway to discovering how the enemy targets believers' minds to keep them in bondage. When he can keep us in bondage, we feel as if we are unworthy to receive the calling God has on our lives. We don't feel as if we have the knowledge, freedom, or empowerment to pray effectively and war in the spirit realm.

When we are attacked with negative thoughts, emotional ailments, and fear, we are in a battle of good against evil—the good in us, the Holy Spirit within us, against evil spirits attempting to deploy against our destinies. There is a constant war, whether or not we see or feel it.

I quoted this passage earlier, but it bears repeating because Scripture discusses the battle of the mind so clearly here:

> For though we walk in the flesh, we do not war according to the flesh. For the weapons of our warfare are not carnal, but mighty through God to the pulling down of strongholds, casting down imaginations and every high thing that exalts itself against the knowledge of God, bringing every thought into captivity to the obedience of Christ.
>
> —2 Corinthians 10:3–5

The Complete Jewish Bible reads:

> For although we do live in the world, we do not wage war in a worldly way; because the weapons we use

> to wage war are not worldly. On the contrary, they have God's power for demolishing strongholds. We demolish arguments and every arrogance that raises itself up against the knowledge of God; we take every thought captive and make it obey the Messiah.

I love how the Jewish translation states to "take every thought captive and make it obey the Messiah." This is an excellent, practical exercise you can apply daily. Does the thought that penetrates my mind obey the Messiah? Does this idea follow the Messiah and align with the Word of God? Life applications such as these can assist you in conquering every thought.

Prophetic Exercise: Capture the Lie

What thoughts have you entertained that do not align with the Messiah? Write down the thoughts now and rebuke them. Speak out and declare, "I rebuke the thought, lie, or vain imagination that penetrates my mind regarding [insert something from your list]." Tell the thought, lie, untruth, or distraction to go in Jesus' name. Right now, break agreement with it! Speak out and declare that you aren't going to listen to the enemy anymore. Come on; get aggressive about it. Break agreement with that thing!

Battle Strategies and Tactics

As we battle and the enemy wages war against us, we need battle strategies and tactics. The Word of God and our minds can be two great tools to have in our arsenals against the demonic world. When we arm ourselves fully with all the weaponry we can, evil spirits won't be able to plague our minds. The Lord told me once, "Kathy, if your mind is full of Scripture, there will be no room in it for the enemy."

We must fight the fires of hell with the fire of the Holy Spirit and the Word of God. Capturing every thought takes practice. I would like to say I was quickly delivered of mind-binding spirits and thoughts that tormented me, but I wasn't. We have to consider that we have years of behavior patterns, habits, and thoughts to undo and renew. When we have a specific way we think, we cannot change that overnight. We must "be transformed by the renewing of your mind" (Rom. 12:2). This verse speaks of not being conformed to this world but being transformed by the renewal of our minds.

We have heard the saying adapted from Scripture, "We are in the world but not of the world." When it comes to thinking, we cannot think as if we are in the world. We need to think as spirit beings. Let's not adapt to the way the world thinks but be unique in our thinking. Being unique in our thinking comes from knowing what the Word says about us and our identity in Christ.

Capturing every thought isn't easy when you feel stagnant or defeated. Unproductive mindsets can become a struggle to conquer. But the good thing about it is that you don't have to do it alone. You have a helper, the Holy Spirit, to assist you in your times of weakness. He is your strength and portion, as is stated in Psalms. "My flesh and my heart fails, but God is the strength of my heart and my portion forever" (Ps. 73:26). Keep Scripture before your eyes, and the promises of the Bible will assist you to walk out and defeat mind-binding spirits.

Helmet of Salvation

We have been given a helmet of deliverance to assist us with the battle in our minds. When we look at the armor of God, the helmet of salvation is the helmet of deliverance. The word *salvation* means deliverance. Therefore, we can interpret the verse, "Take the helmet of [deliverance] and the sword of the Spirit, which is the word of God" (Eph. 6:17). Once again, I will refer to the Complete Jewish Bible for the proper translation of this Scripture: "And take the helmet of deliverance; along with the sword given by the Spirit, that is, the Word of God." I appreciate that the Complete Jewish Bible lists the word *salvation* as "deliverance." When we see Scripture differently and dive into all the prophetic layers, it will become more applicable.

Years ago I wrote an article for *Charisma* magazine, which I am excerpting here.

> The Lord's Word says to "put on the helmet of salvation." Salvation, when studied, means deliverance.
>
> Why does His Word tell us to put on deliverance, and above all, on our head, over our mind? Our Father knew our struggles would be in our mind. Lies, deception and demonic attacks are rooted in a seducing, mind-binding spirit. It gets your thoughts focused in the wrong direction—in fact, an unhealthy and unproductive thought pattern. Our Father created us and knows us intricately. He is also familiar with the devil and his schemes and tactics.
>
> You see, we have an action. We have something to do. We have to put on our helmet of deliverance. He has already given us the helmet of deliverance, but we have to put it on to guard our minds and thoughts

> to be focused on Christ Jesus. We need to put on our helmet of deliverance to have the mind of Christ and His way of thinking since we have the Spirit of God within us.
>
> We need to pause and think as Christ would think, not as our flesh would want to rise up and make us think, or as the enemy would trap us into thinking. We need to walk throughout life and know that strong helmet is over our mind, covered and secured.
>
> The enemy can only penetrate our thoughts as far as we allow him to. We need to get strong like that armor. Picture the fiery darts attacking our shield of faith and our breastplate of righteousness. The first place those darts come in is our minds.[1]

I'll never forget a message I received shortly after posting this article. An elderly lady contacted me and said she had been attacked with fear for nights in her sleep. It was tormenting. Upon reading this article and looking at it in its correct context of being the helmet of deliverance, she was free. She enrolled in all my discipleship classes to learn more and still follows my ministry. She received great freedom in her mind from having this revelation and mind transition.

The Bible tells us that "we have the mind of Christ" (1 Cor. 2:16). We need to transition our thinking so that we have the mind of Christ, which is the way to beat the enemy and the luring spirits he uses to attack us. We need to transition to Christ's way of thinking.

Prophetic Exercise:
Part 1, Visual Assignment

Develop a practical application, a visual exercise that you can use to guard your mind. Here are some examples:

- Picture a judge's gavel smashing down any thought that you are not supposed to allow.
- Picture a chalkboard in your mind, and erase all thoughts that don't align with God's truth.
- Picture the helmet of salvation and deliverance being put on your mind and blocking any arrows from the enemy attempting to invade your thoughts.

Think of an example that will work for you.

Prophetic Exercise: Part 2, Visual Exercises

Here are some visual exercises you could picture in your mind to help you shut down your thoughts, focus, and stop analyzing.

- Picture the helmet of salvation going on your head, and focus on how the strong metal helmet would feel against your forehead. As you focus on the pressure of the helmet visually and mentally, your mind won't be able to process what you were thinking about and it gives you a chance to stop overthinking. The word *salvation* means deliverance. Therefore, think of the helmet as being liberation for your mind.
- Take a moment and imagine your thoughts on a chalkboard, then visualize your arm moving and your hand erasing and cleaning the blackboard. You now have a clean slate for the Holy Spirit to come in with the spirit of revelation. Visual exercises can distract your mind from where it was previously focused.
- A judge's gavel is a powerful tool when it is struck

against a wooden base, making the verdict final. A judge has the final say, and you too have the final say against raging thoughts. Picture a judge's gavel in your mind, striking down those thoughts and throwing them out. I envision the gavel coming down and the thoughts moving to the side and out of my trajectory. You have the authority to issue the final verdict in your mind. Dismiss the case of being overanalytical.

RECOGNIZE THE VOICE OF THE ENEMY

Thoughts run rampant through our minds, but what or who is the source? Knowing who we are listening to is instrumental in capturing thoughts that would hinder our destinies. Recognizing what comes into our minds, how we think, and how God speaks to us will help us to evict anything counterproductive. I wrote a book on this topic titled *Who Is Speaking?* (See the appendix.) It is imperative to clearly and quickly identify whether we are hearing God, the enemy, or our own thoughts and vain imaginations. In the practical application section at the close of this chapter, I will give you exercises to help you determine the source of your thoughts.

Remember, the enemy is the "father of lies" (John 8:44). Recognizing his lies is one of the first steps in exposing him. Have you ever stopped and considered how he speaks to you? What does he say? What tactics does he use to lure you into a mental battle?

The enemy can also counterfeit things the Father does in your life. He will counterfeit spiritual experiences and physical manifestations and make you believe you hear the voice of God, when it is the enemy speaking lies. There are false teachers and false prophets in the world, and whether the enemy speaks through them or to you directly, the Bible warns, "And no wonder! For even Satan disguises himself as an angel of light" (2 Cor. 11:14). Be aware that he is sneaky and crafty. Recognizing the difference between how the Father speaks to you, how you hear yourself think, and how the enemy attacks your mind is crucial to walk in victory over mental ailments.

Break Mental Generational Curses

Depression, mental ailments, stress, anxiety, and worry can be inherited through generational lines. As we are raised and see these emotions and ailments manifest in our loved ones, they can come upon us. The Bible speaks of how generational curses work and travel through bloodlines. (See Numbers 14:18.)

Freedom can manifest completely. We are no longer under the curse. We have been given a new bloodline. But we must destroy negative thoughts in our minds by going to the root source and entry point of those curses.

When I was receiving my freedom, I would renew my mind by telling myself, "I am adopted. I am not a product of my parents. I am a kingdom citizen. I have a heavenly Father who has no curse in Him. Therefore, I am not under a curse." I relied on scriptures such as the following to help me renew my mind:

> For you have not received the spirit of slavery again to fear. But you have received the Spirit of adoption, by whom we cry, "Abba, Father."
>
> —Romans 8:15

> For you did not receive a spirit of slavery to bring you back again into fear; on the contrary, you received the Spirit, who makes us sons and by whose power we cry out, "*Abba*!" (that is, "Dear Father!").
>
> —ROMANS 8:15, CJB

In the New King James Version, Romans 8:15 says we "have received the Spirit of adoption." I utilized this verse when trying to break free from the similar traits I had with my mother. When my mind went in an unproductive direction, I would speak out and decree, "I have received the Spirit of adoption."

Then I went a step further. I thought of verses such as Romans 11:19 and John 15:5, where the Bible speaks of us being branches grafted into the vine. Since my skin is very transparent and I can see my veins, I would look at my veins branching off from other veins as limbs branch off a tree. I thought about all the places they connected to other veins, and I envisioned being connected and grafted to my heavenly Father and Jesus. Whenever I would focus on a generational curse, fear, or mind-binding spirits due to the curse, I would speak out and declare, "I have received the Spirit of adoption. I am not who my parents made me be. I have my heavenly Father's blood running through my veins, and I am a son of God. I have a new bloodline."

Prophetic Exercise:
Prophesy Over Yourself

I prophesied Romans 8:15 over myself. Prophesying over yourself is similar to declaring over yourself. What truth do you need to prophesy to bring your thoughts into the place the Lord intends them to be?

Holy Spirit Conviction vs. Demonic Condemnation

How do you know whether you are hearing Holy Spirit conviction or demonic condemnation? While you learn to conquer every thought, you need to know the source of your thoughts. Taking captive your flesh, thoughts, feelings, and any confusion in your mind is essential.

Holy Spirit conviction

When the Holy Spirit corrects or convicts us, He does it quickly. I like to describe it as the "get in, get out" approach. He will correct, discipline, and show us what we did wrong, and then He will love us. He will show us the mistake, lay it on our hearts to repent and ask for forgiveness, and then He will expect us to move on. He will convict us until we do something about it, and He will always lead us back to God, prompting us to make our relationships with Him right again. We might feel slightly grieved or disappointed, but it will lead us to action and truth. Once it is over, we might think about it for a few minutes and then move on. It's done, it's handled, and we feel released.

When the Holy Spirit gives you conviction or a word of knowledge, it won't leave you until you act on it. The same word will keep coming to you. It is like a BASIC computer program that we used to write years ago. The program tells us what to do line by line, but we always have a "go-to" line in the program. Therefore, no matter what we do, or in this case, what we try to avoid, He will always bring us back to the original instruction.

We can try to ignore it, but the Holy Spirit will bring it to us until the conviction becomes so uncomfortable that we must act on it. As soon as we act on it, we feel released by the Spirit of the Lord and know we have been obedient to what He has called us to do.

Demonic condemnation

Condemnation from the enemy is different. He wants us to sit and think and rot and stink. He will make us feel unworthy and defeated. His goal is to have the emotions of guilt, regret, blame, and shame manifest, causing us to focus on the negative emotions of our mistakes. He wants these emotions to plant seeds inside us telling us that we are no good, that we will mess up again, and that people aren't going to forgive us for our mistakes. The enemy will attempt to twist and turn our thoughts. He will repeat old lies to us and make us feel like we are in the pit with no way out. He wants us to wallow in our self-pity.

I remember years ago when I got mad at someone, I would stay mad for three days and didn't want to let go of it. I think the enemy is similar to that in our lives. He wants us to stay mad, stay in self-condemnation, and not let go of it. I believe this is a key difference between conviction and condemnation—conviction is quick, but condemnation lags. Remember, the thief comes to steal, kill, and destroy (John 10:10), and the very things he wants to steal, kill, and destroy are your time, emotions, and freedom.

Discover the Difference

The next time you can't blow something off, test the source. Ask yourself, "Is this Holy Spirit conviction that will lead me to action and be short and brief, or is the devil sending forth condemnation to make me heavy and keep me in a place of worry and defeat?"

Get in the Word of God and bind your mind to the mind of Christ. (See 1 Corinthians 2:16.) Don't entertain unnecessary thoughts. Don't rent space in your mind to Satan by allowing him to occupy your thoughts.

Prophetic Exercise:
Conquer Your Thoughts

Spend time in prayer and reflect, "Are there times I was convicted versus condemned? How can I learn to hear the voice of the Lord faster?" The next time you get a direction, correction, or instruction, ask yourself, "Where did this come from?" and "How does this make me feel?" When we take things to God in prayer instead of flippantly finding the solution, we will know the true source and how to proceed with what is being presented to us.

The Bible says, "Therefore, my dear brothers, let every person be quick to listen but slow to speak, slow to get angry" (Jas. 1:19, CJB). Let's be quick to discern, slow to react, and cautious before taking in the thought.

It's Time for Activation

It's time to pray and decree your freedom from mind-binding spirits and lies of the enemy.

Prayer of Repentance, Renunciation, and Breaking Agreement

I break agreement with every unproductive and unfruitful thought. I dismiss thoughts that do not align with the Word of God. Every lying, mind-binding, deceptive spirit, I command you to get out of my mind and enter me no more, in the name of Jesus. I repent of self-pity, emotional bondage, and feeling defeated in my thoughts. I rebuke and destroy every demonic stronghold in my mind. I renounce and break agreement with fear, stress, worry, anxiety, rejection, trauma, torment, and unworthiness. I command every evil infiltration in my thoughts and luring, seducing, mind-binding spirits to go now. Get out of my mind in Jesus' name.

IMPARTATION AND ACTIVATION PRAYER

I thank You, Lord, that I have the mind of Christ. I receive the Word of God in my life and call it forth to full activation. I thank You that I am created in the image of my Father God, and therefore I am empowered to conquer every distracting thought. I receive the fullness of what You want to do in my life. Help me to rise in authority and take every thought captive. In Jesus' name, amen!

PROPHETIC PROCLAMATIONS (FAITH DECLARATIONS)

I redirect any negative and unproductive thoughts! I am disciplined in my thinking!

I take dominion over my mind. Godly thoughts fully occupy my mind!

I proclaim that I will take every thought captive and instantly dismiss from my mind every thought that does not align with Scripture.

I declare and decree that I have the helmet of salvation

and deliverance to help me capture every thought. I am not alone; Jesus is with me to release freedom in my life.

I speak and decree that I have not been given a spirit of fear or intimidation but of power, love, and a sound, self-disciplined, and self-controlled mind (2 Tim. 1:7).

Spiritual Activation

1. Capture your thoughts. When a thought makes you heavy, worried, or fatigued, dismiss it instead of entertaining it. Immediately take the thought captive, and don't allow it a foothold in your mind.
2. Through time with the Holy Spirit, identify and discern your negative thoughts. Categorize which thoughts are fleshly and which thoughts are from demonic lying spirits. Recognize and discern the voices of the enemy, God, and your flesh to know the difference.
3. Do you suffer with fear, anxiety, or depression? Can you identify the root and entry point? Spend time and seek the Holy Spirit for revelation on how to renew your mind. Expect Him to give you a strategy that is unique for you and will click with the way your mind processes information and handles stressful situations.

SPIRITUAL WARFARE DECLARATIONS

In Jesus' name I demolish every principality and stronghold that would come against my mind, and I speak and declare that you will infiltrate my mind no more.

I break agreement and cast out all generational curses of emotional ailments and demonic strongholds. I have been given authority over all things; therefore these hindrances must leave in the name of Jesus.

By the fire of God I incinerate and burn up completely every demonic assignment that has been established against my mind.

I refuse to allow negativity and mind-binding spirits to operate in my life. Every spirit sent to torment me, be still now in Jesus' name.

I break down every negative thought, every spirit of worry and fear, and every destructive spirit, and I tell you to evacuate now in the name of Jesus!

Chapter 10

REBUKE AND EXPOSE DEMONIC ASSIGNMENTS

I DIDN'T GROW UP wanting to be a deliverance minister. I didn't know anything about demons or how they operate. My husband was the pastor of a church when we began to have the paranormal experiences I described earlier in this book. We were thrown into what I call "deliverance boot camp." We encountered Jezebel spirits long before we even knew what they were. People placed literal curses on us at bonfires and séances and trashed our reputation in the community. We were in an all-out war before we knew how to combat spiritual forces. These experiences made us stronger and ready for the call to deliverance ministry that God had placed on my life.

In this chapter I will expose some of the most volatile strongman spirits that I have encountered in ministry. This is not an exhaustive list but a practical starting point in your understanding of strongmen spirits. When Jesus was talking about the strongman, He said to bind it. "How can one enter a strong man's house and plunder his goods unless he first binds the strong man? And then he will plunder his house" (Matt. 12:29). People misinterpret this verse and always want to go after the strongman first.

The Complete Jewish Bible states it as, "How can someone

break into a strong man's house and make off with his possessions unless he first ties up the strong man? After that he can ransack his house." *Ransack*, according to Webster's, is "to search through and steal from in a forceful and damaging way."[1] Visualize someone ransacking a house. He goes through that house like a crazy person, seeking items of value. But the objects of greatest importance are not always the first things discovered. Often the most valued items are hidden or take longer to find.

It is the same way with the strongman, who is of greater value because of keeping people held tightly in bondage. He is hidden and takes longer to discover and expose. We can bind the strongman from activation while we plunder, but we cannot evict it from the premises until we know its characteristics and legal rights. Knowledge of how the strongman operates will help us plunder his goods.

JEZEBEL

Jezebel is the name of a strongman spirit of control. It is named after Queen Jezebel, whose story is recorded in 1 and 2 Kings. Jezebel was evil, vindictive, seductive, and manipulative. She promoted the worship of false gods, being a Baal worshipper, and killed God's prophets. She was prideful and used her beauty to manipulate and seduce people into doing what she wanted. Jezebel was a woman, and even though the Jezebel spirit does primarily function through women, it can also operate through men.

Spirits of control often begin with a generational curse. "The LORD passed by before him, and proclaimed, 'The LORD, the LORD God, merciful and gracious, slow to anger, and abounding in goodness and truth, keeping mercy for thousands, forgiving iniquity and transgression and sin, but who will by no means clear the guilty, visiting the iniquity of fathers on the children and on the children's children, to the third and the fourth generation'" (Exod. 34:6–7). If you want to know how controlling a person is, take a look at their mother and sometimes their father. Often Jezebel spirits arise from having a controlling parent. Control manifests in different ways. I once discovered one of my friends was controlling, but it was subconscious and subtle; you wouldn't identify it as control unless you knew Jezebel's operations.

Jezebel seduces in a manipulative way. When I speak of seduction, it is not necessarily in a sexual way. Jezebel draws and lures you into her plans. She likes to appear as your new best friend, the new super spiritual, super helpful person in a ministry, and she always attempts to get as close to the leader as possible. She will be there when you need someone, give you all her time, and lavish her money on you in an attempt to infiltrate your heart. Her words are seductive and manipulative; she agrees with you to build trust.

Later she overpowers you to bring forth her true motives. She is filled with offense, rejection, and pride, and she will betray you every time to activate her plan. She comes in disguise, prettily packaged, but she is a viper snake out for the kill. A viper keeps its fangs inside its mouth and brings them out at the last moment to inject its deadly venom. Similarly Jezebel is sneaky and stays in disguise until she wants to overpower you. And when she does, her tactics are deadly. She divides ministries, ruins relationships, and closes businesses. She leaves destruction and ruin in her wake.

Jezebel is rebellious, and the Bible says that "rebellion is as the sin of witchcraft" (1 Sam. 15:23). Jezebel is fueled by manipulation, pride, and rebellion. When a person manipulates, he or she says or does something to cause an outcome in that person's favor. Manipulation is rebellion against authority and being cunning and sneaky to get your way. It is a form of witchcraft. Control, rebellion, pride, and manipulation are all sins. They lead to witchcraft and ultimately a strongman spirit of Jezebel operating through a person. It is not enough to pray against the spirit of Jezebel. A person must want deliverance from control, selfishness, and pride.

WITCHCRAFT AND JEZEBEL

Jezebel is a master manipulator and operates jointly with a spirit of witchcraft. Jezebel comes to silence the voice of the prophetic. How can Jezebel silence you? Praying and talking against you, the anointing on your life, and the words you have to speak out releases curses into the spiritual atmosphere. There is power in the words we speak, whether spoken by Christians or the evil forces of witchcraft operating against Christians through false prophets, satanists, witches, and warlocks.

Have you ever been ready to preach or witness to a person, and suddenly you find yourself straining to get out the words or you feel like you are losing your voice? These are attacks of the Jezebel spirit and witchcraft activities against the body of Christ. They can be sent forth purposely by a person or by a principality operating over a territory.

Occult and witchcraft covens serve the enemy and are taught to send forth assignments to hinder your ministry, preaching, prayer life, and teaching. They purposely pray against Christians. They sit in your meetings and pretend to receive the Word, but they are there to pray against you and try to stop God's voice from speaking through you. I have experienced my voice being fine, but suddenly, as I went to preach, my vocal cords felt strained. One time, I was in another country when this happened, and they knew the local witch would be at the meeting. She showed up, and they caught her on video as she actively practiced witchcraft. I got up and took authority over the witchcraft, bound and restricted the activity, commanded my vocal cords to function correctly, and continued with the meeting.

People operating in occult and witchcraft activities look for your possessions to use as a point of contact. Having your property gives them great power in the spirit world because they can touch it physically as they pray curses over it. If you feel someone could curse you through an object or possession of yours, pray against it, cover your possession with the blood of Jesus, and break up the point of contact in the spiritual realm.

Pray on the offense instead of on the defense against witchcraft operations. Ask the Holy Spirit to reveal what is being spoken against you. Seek Him for divine strategies to break up the curses and remove their effect in the spirit realm. If you have uncomfortableness in your spirit about a situation (often called "having a check in your spirit"), it is most likely discernment, and you should take action. Audible prayers, declarations, and decrees are most effective in breaking up curses. You must demolish the spiritual realm with the power of your words. I discuss this topic in depth in the chapter "Spiritual Warfare Is Audible."

SENTINEL SPIRIT

The Bible warns us of false spirits, and the sentinel spirit is a top-ranking counterfeit spirit. When we look in military terms defined in the *American Dictionary of the English Language*, a *sentinel* is "a soldier sent to watch or guard an army."[2] The sentinel spirit is a false spirit that enters a person's soul and sets up guard. The New King James Version calls this a "different spirit."

> For if he who comes preaches another Jesus whom we have not preached, or if you receive a different spirit which you have not received, or a different gospel which you have not accepted—you may well put up with it!
>
> —2 CORINTHIANS 11:4, NKJV

The sentinel is a false spirit that mimics the Holy Spirit. The Holy Spirit gives us a prayer language in which to speak and pray out. However, the sentinel spirit attempts to imitate everything God does. In the Old Testament we see examples of how magicians replicated acts of God. In Exodus 7 the Lord turned Aaron's rod into a serpent and turned the water into blood. But Pharaoh's magicians did the same acts.

Have you ever been around someone whose prayer language—the tongue in which the person spoke—seemed off? Maybe you had a check—an uncomfortableness—in your spirit that something wasn't right. The enemy has a language too and can make a person's speech sound like tongues. The sentinel spirit manifests a false spirit of tongues through a person.

Christians who have this sentinel spirit can have a false tongue. The demons that infiltrate their souls can arise and speak a tongue, just as a demon can take over a person's voice and you hear a demon speak out of the person's mouth. Usually Christians do not know that a false spirit occupies them. Ministry leaders can sometimes identify something off about the person; however, the person is labeled as being high maintenance because the sentinel spirit is not exposed and identified. The person is shrugged off as a victim or someone who doesn't know how to help himself.

Ministry leaders are under such demand and time constraints that they don't take the time to pray and seek the Holy Spirit. Instead the person is further rejected when the leader doesn't have time to love and genuinely invest in the person and help him or her with the situation. I often have people tell me how they have been to so many other deliverance ministries and churches and how they are often shunned. No one ever went deep enough to release the counterfeit spirit inside them.

Sentinel spirits can enter through false teachings and false prophecies. They manifest more prominently in certain ethnicities and come from ancestry. Ancestral spirits—nationalities that have set up false idols and have evil spirits that travel the generational line—can cause a sentinel spirit to invade a person. People who have participated in voodoo, rituals, satanism, and other forms of witchcraft are primary targets of the sentinel spirit. It is a high-ranking demon and challenging to expel.

When seeking deliverance or trying to evict the sentinel demon, prayer and fasting will be necessary. It is also essential to discover the demonic entity's root cause and legal rights to close all entry points. This demon may not always come out the first time, and multiple encounters with it may need to be attempted to evict it. When deliverance happens, if the person prays in an unknown language, they can and will notice their prayer language change to one inspired by the Holy Spirit.

LEVIATHAN

The strongman of pride is called Leviathan. Leviathan is referred to in the Bible as a huge sea creature. (See Isaiah 27:1.) When we look at the spirit of pride, it is huge and has many facets. Lucifer fell because of pride.

> How are you fallen from heaven, O Lucifer, son of the morning! How you are cut down to the ground, you who weaken the nations! For you have said in your heart, "I will ascend into heaven, I will exalt my throne above the stars of God; I will sit also on the mount of the congregation, in the recesses of the north; I will ascend above the heights of the clouds, I will be like the Most High."
>
> —ISAIAH 14:12–14

Lucifer allowed pride to get the best of him. He felt superior and that he knew best. We encounter many people in and out of the church today who think the same way. Knowing how pride operates will assist us in identifying and exposing this spirit.

IDENTIFY AND DIFFERENTIATE PRIDE

Natural pride

This is pride that we can see and know we have. We are proud of our accomplishments. We like our homes and feel successful in our careers. You are pleased with the way you look and how you raised your children.

Spiritual pride

This pride is blinding and binding. People with pride don't realize they have pride. When you are bound with a spirit of pride, it doesn't want you free, so one of its tactics is to paralyze you spiritually to prevent you from discovering you have a problem.

Exposing pride will bring freedom in your life. Pride's chief accomplishment is to twist and turn communication. Have you ever been in a conversation that could be described as "he said, she said"? In other words, you had a conversation but the person you conversed with later disagrees with you or misstates what you said. You feel the person has put words in your mouth or twisted your meaning. This is pride at its best. The demons of pride cause the hearer to receive a different message and incite a battle between what was said and heard, between what was perceived and what was fact. This breakdown of communication causes discord, offense, and rejection.

Pride works closely with control, offense, and rejection. When pride collaborates with other demonic entities, it builds a strongman, and the strongman of pride is Leviathan. Pride is difficult to deliver because it is blinding. People can't see it in themselves and often say they are not prideful. I remember being told that I was prideful. I kept saying, "No, I'm not." One day the blinders came off, and I saw the pride I was manifesting. I couldn't believe that even though I was a deliverance minister, freeing other people of pride, I couldn't see it in myself. I was so blinded by it spiritually and emotionally. I am thankful that I had that experience because now I have an understanding of how blinding it is.

Pride is a low-level demon that attacks everyone. When a person has operated in pride over the years, it becomes a strongman of Leviathan. Remember, the biblical description of Leviathan is a sea serpent. Pride in the hierarchy of the demonic realm is attached to high-ranking marine spirits. Marine spirits are also related to spirits of witchcraft. Years ago the Holy Spirit revealed to me that above these three spirits is a spirit of Lucifer. It is named after the devil, who used to be called Lucifer.

Python

Have you ever wondered why you couldn't press through to your breakthrough or get your spiritual walk back to where you want it? Our lack of spiritual desire can be more than flesh or laziness. It can be a principality and power in operation! A python spirit is a witchcraft operation coming against your spiritual walk.

> On one occasion, as we went to the place of prayer, a servant girl possessed with a spirit of divination met us, who brought her masters much profit by fortune-telling. She followed Paul and us, shouting, "These men are servants of the Most High God, who proclaim to us the way of salvation."
>
> —Acts 16:16–17

The word *divination* in Greek is referred to as a python.[3] A python spirit in the spiritual realm would correlate to a python snake in the natural. A python kills its prey by constriction and asphyxiation. Constriction is a narrowing or tightening. Asphyxiation is being deprived of oxygen, which can result in unconsciousness or death. The python spirit constricts and tightens around the trachea and makes it difficult to breathe.

When you are in a territory dominated by witchcraft or have a prophetic voice and message, you may feel your trachea tighten. Python spirits generally want to make you prayerless, and they come to attack your spiritual walk. They make you lose your passion for worship, prayer, and the Lord. A python spirit attacks your spiritual walk, and you think you are in a dry place. The python spirit will continue to attack until you eradicate it through prayer.

Constricting is putting pressure on something to make it tighter and narrower. In the natural we lose our voices when our vocal cords are inflamed or swollen, making a narrow passage between them. When this happens, our vocal cords don't vibrate as easily, which inhibits us from talking and speaking fluently. When we look at the spiritual realm, the python and witchcraft spirits do the same to Christian ministers. They come to disrupt and silence the prophetic voice, attempting to inhibit the Word of God from going forth to advance the kingdom of God.

The strongmen spirits exposed in this chapter often work together. Don't assume you are up against one strongman only. There can be many strongmen. In Mark 5 Jesus asked the demon its name, and it said, "My name is Legion; for we are many" (Mark 5:9). I once delivered a lady who had five strongmen of control. Therefore, don't assume anything in the ministry of deliverance and spiritual warfare. Allow the Holy Spirit to prophetically lead you through each situation for what is uniquely needed for that particular circumstance.

It's Time for Activation

Let's pray to break free from demonic strongholds.

Prayer of Repentance, Renunciation, and Breaking Agreement

Heavenly Father, please forgive me for control, pride, and strongholds of the mind. Forgive me for feeling superior over others, releasing word curses in the spiritual realm, or acting out in rebellion, which is the sin of witchcraft. Jesus, I repent. I thank You for what You did on the cross and receive full reconciliation. I break agreement with works of the flesh, wrong attitudes, superiority, generational pride, and Jezebel spirits. I speak and decree that I am forgiven and set free by the blood of Jesus.

Impartation and Activation Prayer

Holy Spirit, fill me with knowledge of the spiritual realm. Be my Leader and Guide. I want to partner with You to help combat the powers of darkness. Help me to walk in the Spirit and not the flesh. Guide me and help me so I don't lean on my own understanding but rely on the Scriptures and prophetic insights You give me. I invite You to lead me in everything I do. Help me to be Spirit led.

Prophetic Proclamations (Faith Declarations)

I speak and pronounce that I am submissive and humble. I have a heart for the Lord.

Thank You, Lord, that I am love because You are love

and Your Spirit lives in me.

I call forth the manifest possession of my destiny. I am ready to embrace my full calling.

I thank You that the kingdom of God is working on my behalf! I know You have every good and perfect gift for me.

I announce that I am free from demonic strongholds. I am effective and useful for the kingdom of God.

Spiritual Activation

1. Identify Jezebel. She has many different characteristics. Heighten your discernment by diagramming her traits, even going as far as to begin to discern people around you who may be manifesting a Jezebel spirit.
2. Discern prophetic words given to you. Is there a wrong word that you were given or something that didn't sit right in your spirit? Try to remember how you received the word—where you were, what the surroundings were. Do you feel you could have received a false word or teaching?
3. Pride twists and turns communication. I say people wear pride on their sleeves. Can you identify anyone with pride, and what are the specific characteristics? How can you check yourself and hold yourself accountable

to make sure you don't manifest those symptoms?

Spiritual Warfare Declarations

I confine and restrain all witchcraft activities. I nullify every evil perpetrator's agenda against me.

I evict every spirit of pride from my soul. Spirit of Leviathan, I command you out now in Jesus' name. I break agreement with pride and deactivate every entry point.

I break agreement with every spirit of control. I paralyze Jezebel's powers and actions over my home, family, ministry, and employment. I restrict Jezebel from operating through my family line.

In the name of Jesus I eradicate and completely abolish every false teaching and false prophecy in my life, and I speak and decree that evil spirits are evicted from my soul and false prophecies do not manifest.

I proclaim every evil spirit is exposed and that hidden agendas are brought forth into the light.

Chapter 11

REBUKE THE ENEMY

In general, most deliverance ministry and spiritual warfare prayers fall short of what we need to bind, restrict, clean up, and clear up in the spiritual atmosphere. People stay in bondage because we don't go deep and far enough in authority and casting out demons. We get bored and stagnant in our prayer time and don't partner with the Holy Spirit to listen to what He says needs to be prayed out. I remember a person who kept trying to take charge of her child's health by praying in her mind, "I rebuke you, Satan." I was trying to impart how to speak out and decree into her situation, but she persisted that rebuking the devil in her mind was enough.

There are two issues with this, and they need to be addressed differently.

1. The devil cannot hear what we think or pray to God silently. Therefore the demonic realm activating orders against this child was not hearing the mother's authority over the child.
2. The second issue was not knowing the application of the word *rebuke*. *Rebuke* means to take authority over something. When we rebuke

> something, we need to take authority over it and then give it a follow-up command.

In the Scriptures, when Jesus rebuked, He gave the item He rebuked a follow-up command. When we look at the storm on the water in Mark 4, we see an example of Jesus rebuking the wind and speaking to the sea. "He rose and rebuked the wind, and said to the sea, 'Peace, be still!' Then the wind ceased and there was a great calm" (Mark 4:39).

Jesus rose and rebuked the wind, which was disrupting the sea. When He rebuked the wind and took authority over it, He spoke to the sea with a follow-up command to be still. Notice that the wind ceased first, as He began His rebuke, the starting point of authority. The wind and the sea—both things He took authority over—had to react for the stillness to come forth. It was twofold: rebuking and speaking a follow-up command.

We discover another example of rebuking when Jesus took authority over demons. "When Jesus saw that the people came running together, He rebuked the foul spirit, saying to it, 'You mute and deaf spirit, I command you, come out of him, and enter him no more'" (Mark 9:25).

The demon did not come out just by Jesus rebuking it. He took authority over the foul spirit, addressing it by name and commanding it to depart and not reenter. He rebuked and then followed up by commanding it to leave and enter no more. He was taking care of the immediate situation and preventing future movement.

When searching through the Scriptures for spiritual warfare techniques, we need to pay attention to words such as *saying*, *said*, and *call*. We need to look for action words in the Scripture. Look again at what Jesus said in Mark 9:25:

"You mute and deaf spirit, I command you, come out of him, and enter him no more." Jesus not only cast the demon out but took authority, commanded departure, and sealed in the person's deliverance by commanding the demon to enter him no more. He rebuked and took complete authority over every part of the demonic stronghold.

We must follow Jesus' example. Direct the demonic realm through commanding. Decree and take authority to demolish attacks. In my book *SPEAK OUT*, you will find a list of powerful, authoritative words and their definitions to use in your prayer time. (See the appendix.) I recommend that you use a variety of words in prayer. This practice can help you avoid a boring, stagnant prayer life. You also have to be careful not to be legalistic in your prayers. When you pray out loud, the enemy can hear your prayers, and he can tell when you are being legalistic and praying routinely instead of inspired by the Holy Spirit and releasing your authority.

Allow the Spirit to Lead

Jesus was not traditional or legalistic. He did not repeatedly minister the same way. The Spirit of God led Him. This book's main message is to be led by the Holy Spirit in warfare, releasing prayer and receiving discernment. I like to say, "Deliverance is not a cookie-cutter ministry. It is not one-size-fits-all." What works for one person doesn't necessarily fit for another.

Jesus delivered in different ways. He conducted warfare through His own prayers, not through another person's prayers. I have discovered that in the body of Christ we want others to fight our battles more than we want to fight them ourselves. We need to learn to pray as Jesus did. Spiritual warfare, being prophetic, and releasing the ministry of deliverance are the most unusual and nonuniform ministries. We can't expect and teach a pattern or formula. We must allow our spirit man to be Spirit-led and instruct us how to release the ministry for each particular situation we encounter.

Jesus Preached and Rebuked Demons

Deliverance and taking authority over demons was the first ministry Jesus released after calling His disciples. In Mark, Jesus dealt with a man in the synagogue who had an unclean spirit. When Jesus preached with authority, He accompanied His preaching by rebuking demons.

> In their synagogue there was a man with an unclean spirit. And he cried out, "Leave us alone! What do You have to do with us, Jesus of Nazareth? Have You come to destroy us? I know who You are, the Holy One of God."
>
> Jesus rebuked him, saying, "Be silent and come out of him!" When the unclean spirit had convulsed him and cried out with a loud voice, it came out of him.
>
> —Mark 1:23–26

Jesus rebuked the demon by telling it to be quiet, and then He gave it a follow-up command to come out. He didn't converse with the demon but took authority to lead the demon into obeying His commands. The demon resisted but had to leave. Mark chapters 1, 5, and 9 have several accounts of Jesus confronting the demonic that give us biblical examples and instructions. In chapter 9 we see another account of the ministry of deliverance.

> When Jesus saw that the people came running together, He rebuked the foul spirit, saying to it, "You mute and deaf spirit, I command you, come out of him, and enter him no more."
>
> The spirit cried out and convulsed him greatly. But it came out of him, and he was as dead, so that many said, "He is dead."
>
> —Mark 9:25–26

Convulsed is defined as a violent, involuntary contraction. It is to contort, shake, or thrash. The demon screamed audibly and shook the boy's body uncontrollably. When we look back at verses 20–22, we discover that the father told Jesus this demonic torment had gone on since his son's childhood, throwing him into the fire and water to kill him. Jesus exuded authority as He commanded the demon to leave and enter him no more (v. 25).

Prophetic spiritual warfare is taking natural knowledge and partnering with the Holy Spirit for Him to tell us what to say in a particular situation. I recall one time during a deliverance session when a man's jaw locked down as a demon manifested. The man couldn't speak but was able to signal me that his jaw was locked. I didn't know what to do next, and I decided to prostrate myself before the Lord for wisdom and direction. He directed me to where this man's wife was waiting. The Holy Spirit revealed to me through a conversation with this man's wife that his uncle had put vows and oaths from Masonry on him. I broke the vows and oaths off his life and cast out the correlating demons. As a result his jaw opened, and he was set free.

I am often asked where to send demons, how they come out, what if they resist, and whether to consult with a demon.

Being prophetic is not concerning ourselves with all these things but trusting the Holy Spirit to lead us. How can you combat warfare if you can't trust the One who knows the way out of that warfare?

In addition to following the Spirit's leading, we need to follow Jesus' example in Scripture. When Jesus dealt with demons, He told them to be quiet (Mark 1:25) and forbade them to speak (Mark 1:34). He did not need to consult with a demon to evict it. Rebuke is taking authority over a demon, not bargaining, arguing, or consulting with it. Your words are prophetically assigned to hit a target. Demons must bow to the name of Jesus and the authority you exude.

REBUKE THE ENEMY OVER YOUR MIND

I've discussed having the mind of Christ already in this book. It cannot be overstated: engaging in prophetic spiritual warfare is taking control and authority over your mind. The enemy attempts to permeate our minds several times a day. When the enemy occupies your mind, it can become difficult to hear from the Spirit of the Lord.

We must not allow fear, trauma, torment, depression, and mental instabilities to occupy our minds or allow the enemy to drag us down into worry, defeat, and anxiety. The transformation of our minds must result in prophetic minds filled with the Spirit of the Lord, a Spirit not of heaviness but of freedom. Every place we do not capture lies, worry, or fear, we entertain them.

We want the Spirit to give us knowledge, but our thinking gets clouded when we allow thoughts to consume us that are contrary to the Word of God. Rebuking the enemy over mind-binding spirits is the beginning of freedom, and when we have freedom, we can hear from the Holy Spirit. I discuss mind-binding spirits more in several episodes of my podcast, *Prophetic Spiritual Warfare*. (See the appendix.)

We desire to rebuke the enemy and take authority over principalities to set people free. Still, the truth of the matter is that we have to begin with ourselves. We have to take authority and rebuke the enemy from our minds. I do this several times a day. Once you have a strongman, it will attempt to invade and victimize you again. Therefore you have to be alert, recognize his tactics, and constantly capture and dismiss thoughts that are not from God. Rebuke the enemy by praying on the offense instead of the defense. Be proactive, and put him under your feet.

Rebuking the enemy in your mind follows the same format Jesus used when rebuking. You will rebuke the thought, capture it, and dismiss it. You will tell the thought to be still, get out, and whatever else you need to say. After rebuking and taking authority, Jesus gave a follow-up command. You will tell the thought to leave, the lying spirit to subside, and the demon to get out. Follow up the expelling of the thought and demonic entity with a truth you can believe, claim, and trust.

Prophetic Exercise: Prayer of Possession

I am more than a conqueror in Christ Jesus. I have a royal inheritance and am loved by my Father God. I am blessed in my coming and blessed in my going. I am rich in the abundant love of the Lord. I have everything I need in Christ Jesus. All things are working together for my good. I have victory over every demonic stronghold and I walk in joy, peace, and love.

Take Authority and Rebuke

We need to be mindful of the kingdom and take authority by rebuking the enemy. In the following Scripture verses Peter was more concerned about the comfort of the world than advancing the kingdom of God. Peter didn't want the Lord to have to go to the cross, but Jesus rebuked Peter for not being mindful of the kingdom.

> Then Peter took Him and began rebuking Him, saying, "Far be it from You, Lord! This shall not happen to You."
>
> But He turned and said to Peter, "Get behind Me, Satan! You are an offense to Me, for you are not mindful of the things that are of God, but those that are of men."
>
> —Matthew 16:22–23

Many times, we don't rebuke the enemy because, like Peter, we are concerned with this world's affairs. There is a saying, "Be bold but controlled." We need to be bold. We can't always be controlled. The church has taught us to preach love, and while that is important, it isn't the only message that should be taught. We must also learn how to bind the enemy by praying authoritatively. We hold back in our prayers and rebukes because we fear what others will think. We need to be so radical for Christ and His kingdom that we don't care what other people think.

I am not suggesting that we act recklessly, but we can no longer allow intimidation to hold us back. If we are praying for someone and need to rebuke the enemy over that person's life, but we are afraid of what the person believes or what he will think, we are doing the person a disservice by not setting him free because of fear of man. We need to realize that it is exactly what he needs, but he doesn't know how to ask for it or receive it. Our actions and heart should be kingdom focused. The concerns and affairs of this world should be second to promoting the kingdom. Being kingdom directed means to rebuke and take authority over anything contrary to the kingdom.

Jesus said, "Get behind Me, Satan!" (Matt. 16:23). Jesus was taking authority over Peter's distraction and detour to His destiny. Some of you need to say, "Get behind me, Satan!" to your situation. You need to speak out and rebuke distractions, delays, and detours to your destiny. You can't wait for everyone else to rebuke the devil on your behalf. Jesus said, "I give you authority" (Luke 10:19), which means you have more authority over your circumstances than those whom you ask to pray for you and rebuke the devil on your behalf. You have authority. Take it!

Prophetic Exercise: Rebuke the Enemy

Don't wait another moment. Be so desperate for freedom that you want to do it now! Activation is instant! Get up and tell the enemy, "I rebuke you," and then speak out and declare what you need him to desist from in your life.

It's Time for Activation

It's time to speak out and rebuke the enemy in your life.

Prayer of Repentance, Renunciation, and Breaking Agreement

Father, forgive me for any arrogance and pride in thinking I knew how to pray better than someone

You put in my life to teach me more intense strategies. Forgive me for any self-exaltation and for feeling all knowing, as if I did not have more places I could grow in the spirit. I break agreement with any unteachable spirit or lack of motivation to press into the Word of God further and learn new prophetic layers of the Scriptures. I renounce any fleshly emotions that keep me from learning, growing, and activating.

Impartation and Activation Prayer

Holy Spirit, help me to receive new revelation. I receive the fullness of God in my life. I activate the kingdom inside me and manifest it. I speak that I am kingdom minded, fulfilling every mission and calling You have for me. I desire to receive my prophetic destiny in fullness with no hindrances. Help me to be fully equipped to exude everything You have so joyfully given me. In Jesus' name, amen!

Prophetic Proclamations (Faith Declarations)

I speak, and the enemy must be bound, be restricted, and carry out any follow-up orders I give him. I have the authority Jesus gave me!

My destiny is going forth unhindered. Familiar seasons, cycles, and spirits of the past have been canceled and nullified in Jesus' name.

Failure is not my portion. Defeat is not an option. I have been given abundant life, love, and power!

I am redeemed from the curse because Christ hung on the cross for me. Therefore I am an overcomer and have victory.

I confess that I am willing to submit to the Holy Spirit and allow Him to correct, convict, and teach me.

Spiritual Activation

1. Change your thoughts. You have a responsibility to change your thoughts. Where do you need to change your thinking, and how can you make a plan of action to implement it?
2. Change your prayers. Where have you possibly prayed amiss, and where do you need to change what and how you are praying to receive effectual results?
3. Rebuking the enemy comes from speaking out. Write a ten-sentence declaration to rebuke the enemy, and take full authority over him.

Spiritual Warfare Declarations

In Jesus' name I eliminate every demonic power from infiltrating my soul with emotional bondage. I am healed and delivered by the blood of the Lamb.

I close entry doors and access points that give legal rights to demonic attacks.

I rebuke every health ailment in my life, and I command my body to align with the Word of God.

I rebuke every evil perpetrator against my finances. I command familiar spirits attacking my finances to be bound and restricted. You will abort your mission to steal my finances.

I uproot every strongman spirit that has infiltrated my soul because of sins I have committed. Strongholds and strongmen, be loosed, in the name of Jesus.

Chapter 12

ACTIVATE YOUR SPIRITUAL SENSES

THE NUMBER ONE question I receive in my ministry is how to increase in discernment and see into the spiritual realm. When people ask this question, I often ask them why they want to see in the spiritual realm and what they will do with the information they receive through discernment. Seeing into the spiritual atmosphere is a blessing; however, seeing in the spiritual realm can also be one of the greatest challenges you will encounter.

It comes down to what you are going to do with the information you receive. I've seen into the spiritual realm for years. The challenge is that when you see a demon on someone's back in a store, you can't go up to the person and say, "Excuse me. I see a demon on you. Can I kick it off you quickly?" A challenge I often face is not enjoying a vacation or a date night out with my spouse. The demonic activity in the atmosphere often rears its ugly face, and I am confronted with the powers of darkness invading my space. I remember going on a date night once with my husband and asking the Lord in advance to turn off my ability to see into the spiritual realm so I could enjoy the evening like a normal person.

I don't regret at all being able to see into the spiritual realm. It has set many captives free and has been a blessing to tell people when I see angels around them. However, it can also be a distraction and make something you once enjoyed challenging to experience. It can make you extra cautious and prayerful about where you go and when. So yes, it is an honor to be in warfare on behalf of the King, but you need to count the cost going in.

Discernment comes in two forms: general discernment, which anyone can function in, and the gift of discernment.

General Discernment

Natural discernment can come from our knowledge, wisdom, and indicators of what will happen next. We may be able to predict a person's actions or motives, such as when moms know their children so well that they can predict what they will do next. By becoming familiar with people, we can anticipate their next move or what they may or may not say or do. General discernment can come from what we know about a situation, the information we have gained, or a perception of what will happen next. Common sense can also have a factor in discernment. Not all discernment is from the Spirit of the Lord; some of it is logical.

The Gift of Discernment

Discerning of spirits is a gift according to 1 Corinthians 12. It is the ability to discern between the Holy Spirit, evil spirits, and the human spirit. The Holy Spirit gives gifts, but we can also increase and stir up the gifts (2 Tim. 1:6). As we utilize a gift, we can grow and increase in the gift. In the gift of discerning of spirits, you have the ability to discern true and false intentions in a person, sense demonic activity or evil spirits in a person, and receive direction from the Holy Spirit for how to proceed in a ministry meeting or natural situation. Additionally you could also have the ability to see in the spiritual realm both angels and demons.

Inward Activation

We can increase our discernment and receive spiritual guidance and understanding. One of the ways we can grow in natural discernment is by people watching. Go to the mall or a busy public place, and people watch. Focus on what people are doing and occasionally see whether you can predict their next moves. Home in on them with your eyes, not physically making eye contact but focusing your eyes on them, and see if you can discern anything about them. You can even do this with people you know at a dinner table or in a Bible study. While focusing on them, concentrate.

There are two ways you can proceed after you are focused on them. The first way is to stay in tune with what you are focusing on but don't think about it. In other words, don't try to figure it out. Focus. Allow the Holy Spirit to speak to you about them. The second way is to ponder, think, and try to figure it out. Put different scenarios forth and see what resonates with you and witnesses in your spirit. Both of these exercises will increase your discernment and activate the prophetic inside you.

Outward Activation

Let the Holy Spirit be your guide, and follow His leading as you seek to go from inward activation to outward activation. This is where you take it a step further. When you are out running errands or people watching, ask the Holy Spirit to give you a prophetic assignment. Then be ready to speak out when you sense His leading.

For example, if I am clothes shopping and feel led to pray, prophesy, or minister prophetic evangelism, I position myself near a person flipping through a rack of clothes and use the clothing as a conversation starter. As the person responds, I ask the Holy Spirit to help me discern her response.

The leap of faith is trusting that after you step out and open your mouth in the natural, the Holy Spirit will do something in the supernatural and give you the words to speak and prophetic insight about the person's situation. This outward activation of your spiritual senses starts with stepping out in faith and boldness. You do something in the natural and expect the Holy Spirit to show up and show off, in a good way, such as downloading information only He knew about the person to get her attention and get her eyes focused on the Lord.

Prophetic Exercise: Inward and Outward Activation

Practice the inward and outward activation techniques I have mentioned to increase your discernment. You will never know whether you are right unless you attempt to release what the Spirit has given you. We often become stagnant in our giftings because we don't release them. By stirring, releasing, and activating our gifts, we can grow in confidence in what God has given us, and we can rely on Him to receive it and release it. I can't tell you how many times I needed to be pushed or needed someone to propel me as I was getting started, but it all begins with a conscious act of obedience.

Listening Prayer

Try listening during prayer, and then act on the words of knowledge you receive. This is a great test to increase your discernment and tune your ear to the voice of the Lord. By yourself or with a group of friends, pray and expect to receive words of knowledge to release to people. The Holy Spirit can tell you what store to go to and what the person will be wearing. Sit and receive from the Spirit by praying in tongues, calling forth words of knowledge, or sitting in silence and waiting for Him to impart something.

Take the information you receive and act on it. Go to the place and look for the person the Spirit described. Approach the person as led by the Holy Spirit. Ask Him to deposit further instructions into your spirit.

**Prophetic Exercise:
Receive a Word of Knowledge**

Stop reading, and spend three to five minutes in silence right now. Be quiet. Try not to think. Just wait patiently on the Holy Spirit and see whether He will give you a word of knowledge or speak to you.

Obedience and Benefits of Increasing in Discernment

I could share many stories of the ways the Holy Spirit has led me to minister to people over the years. For example, I remember a ministry trip that the Holy Spirit had called us to take where He had given us specific travel directions, leading us to Georgia. Then we got a word of knowledge to go to a specific chain restaurant. There were three close by, and we sought to discern which location. The first time we were wrong. We located the other two sites and proceeded.

At the second location we knew the manager was our target. She was working at a nearby table and commented, "I wish the internet would work." My assistant and I instantly slid our chairs over and said, "We can help you with that." We prayed, and the internet began working. However, that was the opener, not the appointment. The manager had prayed and fasted for ten hours the day before and needed to hear a word from the Lord. The Spirit led me to prophesy and speak over her.

Another time, the Spirit of the Lord told me to go with my team to a particular chain store at 2:00 p.m. We obeyed and easily identified whom we sensed the Lord was directing us to approach. We spoke into her life and gave her my card. She called the next day, and we met up with her. She couldn't forgive herself for an abortion and told us she had been planning to commit suicide before we showed up.

And yet another time, I was working in the office when the Lord instructed me to go to our local grocery store. I was busy and trying to ignore it, but the word of knowledge wouldn't leave me. I told one of my team members, and she said, "What are you waiting for? If God is telling you to go, we have to go." We went, and she prayed about what part of the store to go to. She sensed the Holy Spirit telling us to go to the cafeteria.

In the café, people were seated at three tables, but we could not discern which table to approach. Finally I stood up and said, "God told me to come to this cafeteria in this store at this time, and I need to know who needs prayer." At first, people looked at me and said nothing. But then a man interpreted to his friend what I had said and called us over and told us his friend needed prayer.

I share these stories to help you see that your discernment may not be accurate the first time, or you may be tempted to ignore it or doubt that you hear correctly. Moving in the Spirit and trusting Him can be difficult at times. However, trusting the Lord is not contingent on our feelings. Our flesh must be crucified, intimidation must flee, and insecurity cannot be allowed to manifest. Following the Spirit's leading is an act of obedience and discipline on our part. In the examples I shared, I was obedient to carry out the assignment He gave me. But I wasn't the most disciplined in the grocery store's case because I almost missed the appointment. I heard clearly from the Lord, and I should have gone the first time I was asked instead of trying to ignore it.

Confusion in Discernment

Clarity should be present instead of confusion in our prayer times. We can receive an incorrect answer in prayer by thinking about it instead of praying about it. When trying to discern and activate our spiritual senses, we need to be aware of our surroundings, how the enemy can infiltrate our thoughts, where we are, and what we are doing when we receive discernment.

Sadly Christians aren't as disciplined in prayer as we should be. Our prayer times can lack and be passive. We can end up meditating and pondering a decision during our prayer times, and since we are praying, we end up believing the answer is from the Lord when it is not. We need clearly defined boundaries. It is imperative that we differentiate between our own thinking and praying. We can identify hearing from the Lord by making sure we enter His gates with thanksgiving and His courts with praise. (See Psalm

100:4.) When we guard our prayer times and enter through words and songs of praise, we set up a perimeter around our souls that the enemy cannot penetrate.

When we begin our prayer times with thinking and pondering, it can be difficult to make a transition to binding our flesh to connect and hear from the Lord. Our wandering thoughts and what-ifs get involved in scenarios, and often we receive an answer from our thoughts instead of the Lord. If our minds are occupied elsewhere, it can be difficult to focus on what the Lord is speaking. I do not want to argue and say we can't hear from God while driving. I know I have, and I am sure you have, but we are still focused on the road, traffic signs, and pedestrians when we are driving. Therefore we don't have 100 percent of our attention directed toward the Lord and what He wants to speak to us. When we want to pray for something specific and enhance our relationships with the Lord, we need to get in our quiet places without distractions and give Him our full attention.

Downloads of Discernment

Building a relationship with the Holy Spirit and recognizing His voice is instrumental in receiving downloads or what I call "spiritual drops." As we tune our spiritual ears to His voice and build a relationship with Him, He will begin to drop things into our spirits, even when we are not in prayer. There will be times I am walking around the house, and I will get an instruction deposited within my spirit. My daughter Lauren and I both receive drops and downloads. She can ask me a question, and I can instantly receive an answer in my spirit, and vice versa. The Holy Spirit will speak to us clearly and quickly as we enhance our relationships with Him.

In the same way, He can deposit prophetic words and revelation. When you are praying and seeking Him, He will pour out loads of revelation to write down something He wants you to do, or He can give you a prophetic word. You can increase the revelation you receive by spending time in His presence, studying His Word, and getting to know His characteristics and the way He speaks to you.

Increase in Discernment

When the Lord gives you an answer to a question, wait upon Him and see whether you receive further direction. If you are praying for a specific thing and the Lord answers you, then go a step further and pray into the answer, the different directions on how it may manifest. As you pursue Him for more direction, you may see road maps to lead to the solution you are trying to find. You can discover many pieces to the plan God is laying out before you.

Learn how to quiet your mind and focus. It can be challenging to discern when your mind is going in several different directions. You have to give the Spirit a chance to enter your thoughts. If your mind is full of everything else, how will you hear Him when He speaks? Allow Him to penetrate your mind. You might be thinking, "Kathy, He is God. He can penetrate my mind anytime He wants." Really? Is that true? Think about it! Do you give Him a chance, or is your mind going all the time?

I used to be very analytical. The Lord taught me to withdraw and get quiet within myself. I now can be at a conference with noise and people all around, and yet I can connect my spirit to the Holy Spirit, receive instruction, and be in a place of intimacy with Him. This skill assists me in gaining direction for meetings and knowing how the Spirit wants to lead. It takes practice to learn to quiet your soul. Find an exercise or way that you can withdraw and hear from the Lord. I am very visual, so I would do visual exercises in my mind that would clear my thoughts to prepare my mind and heart to hear from the Lord.

Prophetic Exercise: Quiet Your Mind

When your mind is going in several directions, capture the thought. Stop and take a moment and focus on the thought. Take the thought, and envision it moving out of your mind, down your neck, through your chest, and into your heart—into the place of love with the Father. Transfer the busy, analytical thinking from your mind to the place of peace and rest in the Father's love.

If you can, close your eyes and focus on your mind, not the thoughts. Give yourself a focal point, and the thoughts will settle down. Now proceed to draw inner strength from that place of love where the Father is and the Holy Spirit is living inside of you. Set aside the mental and physical distractions from the outside world and draw inward to your spirit man and the Holy Spirit. As you do this, your mind, will, and emotions—the soul part of you—will rely on and get clarity, strength, and revelation from the Holy Spirit. This is the core and essence of this book: partnering with the Holy Spirit. When we submit our souls to the Holy Spirit, we will stop being analytical.

My friends used to label me as the most analytical person they knew. I was a worshipper and still am, but as much as I loved to worship Jesus and focus on loving on Him, distracting analytical thoughts would invade my worship. It would make me leave worship feeling as if I had wasted time because I wasn't focused on the Lord. I became frustrated with myself. As I implemented these practices I have shared with you, I have been able to conquer my analytical thoughts. I believe being analytical is a gift from Father God. It is when we take something good He has given us, mix our flesh in with it, and analyze to the extreme that it can become detrimental to us. You can't remove being analytical fully from your life, but you can minimize it so you can increase in your spiritual walk and enjoy your time in the Lord's presence. Partner with the Holy Spirit, and allow Him to convict you when you are being too analytical.

Five Senses

Where does God best speak to you? You may have a secret place or a place where you best hear from the Lord. Identify this place, position yourself there while growing in discernment, and notice how He speaks to you. This is a time you could try and use your five natural senses to experience the Lord. The five natural senses our Father created—sight, smell, sound, touch, and taste—can also be used to experience God, discern whether demons are present, and sense what is happening in the spiritual atmosphere. Have you ever smelled the presence of God or sensed evil? Have you experienced manifestations using your senses?

Sight

Our Father can open our eyes to see spirit beings in both the natural and spiritual realms. We can see demons and angels. We can also experience visitations from Jesus and the Holy Spirit, where we see them appear in a room. In your quiet time the Lord may appear to you in a vision, or He might appear physically before you. I remember the

Lord appearing to me in an intense vision, taking my hand, leading me up to heaven, and showing me my son who died in my womb.

The Lord can use our eyes to show us when demons are present and when they are gone. He can use our eyes to supernaturally assist us in ministry or teach us how to pray specifically for something. Spiritual sight comes from a place of intimacy and commitment to the Lord.

Smell

We can smell the fragrance of God in our worship or prayer times. Have you ever noticed the smell in the room change and become sweet like roses? When you are in prayer or worship and you suddenly notice a smell sweep into the room, it is the Lord.

I was preaching one time, and I started to smell frankincense and myrrh. It was extraordinarily strong. There was no anointing oil in the room with frankincense and myrrh. I couldn't get past the smell. I closed my folder, paused my teaching, and began to discern.

The Spirit of the Lord instructed me not to touch anyone but to stay sitting on my stool and speak whatever He told me. The next four hours were constant healings, miracles, deliverance, and impartation of the fire and presence of God. Backs were healed, demons were cast out, and people lay in the presence of the Lord.

Sound

Our ears are gateways to the spiritual realm. Our ears can hear in the spiritual and natural. We can hear God when our spirits are connected to His Spirit. God also speaks audibly at His choosing to His people. We can hear another sound if we tune in to it. We can hear the spiritual atmosphere, such as the fluttering of angels' wings, or we can hear a scurrying around in the spiritual realm of demons being activated on assignment.

The Spirit gave my team and me discernment on how the demonic operates through the airwaves and how to bind and restrict demonic chatter and assignments. The airwave declaration He supernaturally downloaded to us is in the front of my book *Discerning and Destroying the Works of Satan*. (See the appendix.)

Taste and touch

We can experience taste and touch in the spiritual. However, unlike the other senses, we will have to press into the spiritual realm a little more to see their manifestations.

Prophetic Exercise: Be Alert and Aware of Your Surroundings

Activate your spiritual senses by becoming aware and alert. Sometimes we get in robot mode in our spiritual walks and can become legalistic in hearing from God and how we experience Him. We need to stretch ourselves to go to another level and expect more. Sometimes, increasing and releasing discernment and a new anointing aren't as hard as we would think. It comes from expecting more, reaching for a new level, and trying. As Christians we can get into false contentment and stagnancy because we are satisfied with what we have or don't know how to aim for more. We should always be reaching for and expecting to go to a new spiritual place, deeper and closer to the Lord.

It's Time for Activation

Pray and activate your spiritual senses.

Prayer of Repentance, Renunciation, and Breaking Agreement

I repent of being frustrated or claiming I did not hear from God. I do hear from the Lord. I renounce any inadequacies in my discernment. I break agreement with comparison to other people and how they hear and receive from the Lord. I renounce feelings I have had when I heard from my flesh or people told me I was wrong. I break the hindrances these words and feelings erected in my life. In Jesus' name, amen.

Impartation and Activation Prayer

I thank You, Holy Spirit, that You desire to partner with me. I want to receive from You. I know You are my friend, and You desire to communicate with me. I open my soul and spiritual senses to hear from You. I will trust You for the revelation that You give me. I will no longer question my discernment but go forth in confidence that I hear from You when I partner with You and keep You first in my life. In Jesus' name, amen!

Prophetic Proclamations (Faith Declarations)

The Holy Spirit is my best friend. He is working on my behalf. He desires to communicate with me. I am sensitive to the Spirit and make time to be in His presence.

The Holy Spirit is my teacher, instructor, and friend. He leads me when I look to Him.

I proclaim the Holy Spirit is my Guide. He gives me revelation and instructs me on what direction to take in my life.

I speak and decree that I receive discernment from the Holy Spirit and that my flesh does not get involved in decisions.

I receive from the Holy Spirit insights and instructions. I am obedient and disciplined to act quickly on the unction He gives me.

Spiritual Activation

1. Make yourself available to the Holy Spirit. How can you remove distracting thoughts and busyness to spend time waiting on Him?
2. Increase your discernment. Do you need to remove doubt or be delivered of something attacking your confidence to hear from God?
3. Position yourself to use your senses. Spend time praying for people and taking in prayer requests to tune your senses into the Spirit of the Lord.

Spiritual Warfare Declarations

I obstruct the enemy from infiltrating my prayer time. I speak and decree that I do not have confusion but clarity, and I can hear from the Holy Spirit clearly.

I restrict evil spirits from penetrating my thoughts. I put on the helmet of salvation and deliverance over my mind.

I obstruct every evil spirit from attacking me and my discernment. I tune my five senses to the spiritual realm, and I am not discouraged, because I hear from the Holy Spirit.

I bind and abolish spirits of fear and intimidation. I have been given love, power, self-discipline, self-control, and a sound mind.

I forbid the enemy from interrupting my time with the Lord and sending forth spiritual attacks to disrupt my God time.

Chapter 13

BREAKING AGREEMENT

Fear was a stronghold in my life for years. I was afraid of being in a vehicle on a bridge with water underneath. I was afraid of heights, storms, and icy, snowy roads. I felt fear when I would hear a slight noise or vibration in my vehicle, thinking something was wrong or I would get in an accident. I paid close attention when something was off in my body, fearing I had a medical ailment manifesting. These fears would bind my mind, traumatize me, and keep me in distress.

Fear gained an entry point into my life as pessimistic people surrounded me—I liken it to being taught to fear. I was taught to think the worst of a situation and to expect a negative outcome. Fear was part of the generational curse I inherited. I was raised in a family where pessimism exceeded optimism. Thinking the worst about a situation was a normal and usual reaction, and it became part of me.

Vain imaginations and false scenarios would run rampant through my mind, causing worry and fear. This followed me into my adulthood because I never received the knowledge that I was fighting spiritual forces. I wasn't taught how to reverse fearful emotions.

As I write this now, I can feel the lure of familiar spirits trying to pull me backward in my thinking. I can sense the spiritual attack that tries to pull my thoughts from writing to focusing on the minuscule physical variations I am experiencing in my body. But it is a lie from the pit of hell, as I am in excellent health! The devil is relentless and will never give up trying to attack.

I was taught to fear sickness, disease, and anything abnormal about my body. As a child I heard negative comments about adverse health manifestations. I heard statements such as, "If you have a heart palpitation, it might be a heart attack," or "If you have recurring headaches, it could be an aneurysm," or "If you have an abnormal mole, it is likely to be cancer."

We know medical symptoms can manifest in our bodies, and some of these situations can happen. But I heard the worst-case scenario every time there was a symptom, even if it wasn't a genuine health concern. Words in our home were exaggerated and taken to the extreme.

The thing about the devil is that even though you may have broken free from strongholds, the enemy will attempt to torment you with the very thing you conquered to try and draw you back into your struggle. The difference for me now is that the enemy has been exposed, and I recognize his lies to seduce me back into bondage. Half of the victory of spiritual warfare is recognizing the attack.

As I entered adulthood, I didn't know I was wrestling with principalities. One challenge of deliverance is not knowing you are in bondage; another is when you discover the bondage but don't know what to do about it. Instead of repenting and renouncing fear, I allowed the lies to penetrate my mind and torment my soul. By not taking authority over the lies, I opened a place in my soul that evil spirits could attack.

Evil spirits had a legal right to harass and invade my soul. Remember, the Bible instructs us, "Submit yourselves to

God. Resist the devil, and he will flee from you" (Jas. 4:7). Submitting to God and resisting the devil take a conscious effort. They take practice and perseverance.

The apostle Paul tells us, "But I fear, lest somehow, as the serpent deceived Eve by his craftiness, so your minds may be corrupted from the simplicity that is in Christ. For if he who comes preaches another Jesus whom we have not preached, or if you receive a different spirit which you have not received, or a different gospel which you have not accepted—you may well put up with it!" (2 Cor. 11:3–4, NKJV). I shared this scripture in a previous chapter because it talks about receiving false teachings and spirits. However, it also speaks to legal rights. When the Corinthians took in the false teaching, they gave "a different spirit" a legal right to be there. Paul told them, "You may well put up with it!" They either opened the door to the false teaching or did nothing about it.

It is the same if we allow the enemy to plague our minds or if we sin but do nothing about overcoming it. We enable what we don't fight against, and it becomes a legal right.

If we don't remove demonic access, we will continue to be tormented and attacked by the enemy. If we don't rebuke the attacks, we agree with the strongholds. Strongholds are not only broken by expelling demons. Changing our thoughts and learning our kingdom citizenship are keys to overcoming penetrating thoughts. Renewing our minds and receiving what the Word of God says about us will crowd out the voice of the enemy.

The Lord told me years ago, "Kathy, if your mind is full of Scripture, there will be no room for fear." Fear is the voice of the enemy. Fear leads us to destructive thoughts, which are death to our souls, but Scripture leads us to life and peace. "Having one's mind controlled by the old nature is death, but having one's mind controlled by the Spirit is life and *shalom*" (Rom. 8:6, CJB). We are responsible for most of our thoughts and vain imaginations that run wild. We have a decision to make when false scenarios, doubt, and fear enter. Are you going to entertain them or dismiss them? Will you get busy and change the negativity, or will you focus on what brings you down?

Close Doors

We cannot effectively fight and battle in the spiritual realm if we are in sin or need to release or receive forgiveness. I'm reminded of Acts 19:15, when the demon said to the Jewish exorcists: "I know Jesus, and I know Paul, but who are you?" They had no authority because they had not received salvation and the power of forgiveness.

When we release forgiveness, repent, and renounce places where we have enabled demonic attacks, we can walk out our freedom and destroy the enemy's legal right to harass us. We must examine our lives and receive deliverance if we want to have authority against hostile attacks. When we live in sin, hold unforgiveness in our hearts, carry a defeated mentality, or languish in prayerlessness, we open gateways to demonic infiltration. Where open doors and legal access points are present, we don't have authority in the spiritual realm. When we open ourselves through sin, we give place to the devil. Remember, the apostle Paul told us, "Do not give place to the devil" (Eph. 4:27). We have legal rights to subjugate the enemy, but when we are in sin, we relinquish the dominion Jesus gave us.

Demons and angels roam the earth. Angels are assigned to protect and guard us. Demons cause spiritual attacks.

Unseen spiritual entities can see us even though we can't see them. The enemy knows what we struggle with and how to attack us. He knows when we are in sin and when we are exuding or yielding authority. In Luke 4:34–35 the demons knew Jesus' authority and had to act on His commands. The opposite is also true: if we don't know our authority or yield it due to sin, we have opened a door and given legal rights to evil spirits. Therefore they are not going to be bound and restricted.

The demonic realm has battle plans written up against you. Evil spirits lurk around you, monitor what you say and do, and use the information they collect to bring evidence against you to demonic hierarchies. You must cut off and evict all access points to the satanic world and the infiltration of attacks the enemy orders to bring your way.

Use the fire of God to burn up the blueprints of hell against you. Self-evaluate, and allow the Holy Spirit to convict, correct, and discipline you. This leads to a life of truth and love, one of purity and honesty with yourself and others. When you get all the junk out of your trunk, you can be useful and effective for the kingdom of God.

Repentance and forgiveness are frontline strategies for living a victorious life and destroying entry points to demonic attacks and strongholds. When sin and flesh manifest, we must break agreement by renouncing, repenting, and removing legal entry points and root causes. We must pray audibly and speak out against these actions, and as we forgive ourselves and others, we can close the door to demonic attacks.

Renounce and Break Agreement

The beginning step to conquering spiritual attacks is to renounce sin and unclean activities in your life. *Renounce* is defined as to disown, to reject, to refuse to own, to cast off, and to renounce allegiance.[1] It is not enough to stop ungodly and unproductive activities and to quit sinning. You must go a step further and break the legal agreement these alliances have created in the spiritual realm. How do you do that? You must proclaim audibly against the legal rights and infiltrations they have created. Serve the enemy eviction notice papers, and tell him to get out of your life. Declare aloud that you are no longer going to participate in activities that prevent you from gaining spiritual ground.

Breaking agreement brings forth deliverance. Confession leads to possession. Confessing and proclaiming your wrongful agreements brings forth freedom. Emotional ailments and strongholds in the flesh and mind must be disengaged.

When I break agreement, I declare, "I do not allow the stronghold to exist." I speak out, "I bind and restrict this action and demonic manifestation in my life." As I proclaim, "I have faith and not fear," or "I am submissive and not rebellious," I announce who I am in Christ. I begin to believe what I speak and decree. I loosen strongholds and obtain freedom.

It is a prophetic proclamation that we disassociate ourselves with the demonic attack, emotional ailments, and demonic infiltrations of our souls. Use the words *I break agreement* when you face a stronghold that does not want to be eradicated from your soul. When you command a demon to get out, but it doesn't leave, you must audibly speak out that you break agreement with the spirit.

Prophetic Exercise:
Breaking Agreement With Strongholds

There is power when we speak out and break agreement with strongholds. We agree with the stronghold by not pursuing our healing and deliverance by being passive, being legalistic, being stagnant, or feeling defeated. Where haven't you been able to experience total victory? What root cause, legal right, or health ailment is plaguing you?

Speaking audibly, repeat this several times right now, "I break agreement with ____________________." Keep doing it until you feel a release, a spiritual shift, or something break. At first you may be repeating this sentence, but keep praying and speaking out until you feel power, authority, and intensity in your words come forth. Believe that you will receive the breakthrough, and make sure after you feel a release to follow up by saying, "I cast out the spirit of ________________"—whatever spirit relates to what you just broke agreement with.

Repentance

Repentance is asking Jesus to forgive our sins. When we repent, we need to search deep within our souls to experience heartfelt sorrow over walking in disobedience toward our heavenly Father. We acknowledge that we were in the wrong and we need to turn away from sin and actions that do not glorify the Lord. Repentance is an act of admitting the regret we feel over past actions. It can manifest in heartfelt cries of our souls when we acknowledge our wrongs.

We repent and ask forgiveness by faith because we know

it is the right thing to do and because we desire to accept the reconciliation that Jesus purchased for us on the cross. Jesus came to give His life for ours. "For the wages of sin is death, but the gift of God is eternal life through Jesus Christ our Lord" (Rom. 6:23). We should have been dead in our sins, but because of Jesus' death on the cross, we will live forever when we accept Him into our hearts and live for Him. *Repent* means to change and turn around. As we decide to live for Jesus and accept the reconciliation of the cross, we turn from our old natures and ways: "...that you put off the former way of life in the old nature, which is corrupt according to the deceitful lusts" (Eph. 4:22).

UNFORGIVENESS: THE TOP LEGAL RIGHT FOR ENEMY ACCESS

Unforgiveness is the top legal right the enemy has to gain access to your life. It is the legal right behind every stronghold and demonic accusation. Jesus spoke about the importance of forgiveness. He put urgency on the ministry of forgiveness because He knew that offering and accepting forgiveness closes the door to demonic attacks. When our hearts hold grudges, offense, and bitterness, we are not living in peace, love, and unity. Open doors to enemy infiltration come forth when we live contrary to the Word of God, and holding unforgiveness does not align with God's Word. When we release forgiveness, as the Bible instructs, we destroy the devil's work over our lives.

Here's what Jesus said about forgiveness:

> Therefore, if you bring your gift to the altar and there remember that your brother has something against you, leave your gift there before the altar and go on

> your way. First be reconciled to your brother, and then come and offer your gift.
>
> —Matthew 5:23–24

> And forgive us our debts, as we forgive our debtors.
>
> —Matthew 6:12

> Then Peter came to Him and said, "Lord, how often shall I forgive my brother who sins against me? Up to seven times?"
>
> Jesus said to him, "I do not say to you up to seven times, but up to seventy times seven."
>
> —Matthew 18:21–22

Unforgiveness is tied to every other demonic stronghold we encounter. When we engage in spiritual warfare but do not receive the full ministry of deliverance, it is often because we hold on to unforgiveness, giving the enemy a legal right to harass us. We need to forgive ourselves and others.

Release Forgiveness

Jesus died on the cross and forgave us. We are to be an extension of the cross and follow His precedent. Extending forgiveness isn't a feeling. If we wait until we feel like it, we might never do it. Extending forgiveness is an action of our hearts. It is saying we acknowledge and accept that Jesus forgave us.

When we hesitate to extend forgiveness, it is often because we feel the other person doesn't deserve it. After all, the person hurt us. We must remember that Jesus forgave us even though we hurt and sinned against Him. He extended His great love to us, and in return for what He did for us, we should release forgiveness to others, whether or not we feel they deserve it. It is an act of releasing agape love, which is God's unconditional love; it is a love of the will, not necessarily of feeling or emotion.

RECEIVE FORGIVENESS

Closing demonic entry points so we can conquer spiritual battles is also contingent on our forgiving ourselves. If we cannot forgive ourselves, there is still unforgiveness in our hearts. We can get stuck in the past, with feelings of unworthiness, shame, guilt, and regret. Holding on to unproductive and unfruitful feelings leads us to establish strongholds in our lives. Over time emotional ailments we don't receive healing for will build up to strongholds that we no longer know how to release. The problems become much bigger than we ever intended.

Our freedom must begin with ourselves. Inner healing—healing that needs to occur within our souls—and deliverance are lifelong processes. As we seek the Holy Spirit through silent meditation, He will reveal issues we need to address, help us remove legal rights, and establish healing where there are soul wounds.

No sin is too big for the Lord to forgive. However, somehow, we perceive that our sin is worse than that of others. We keep ourselves in a prison of shame, guilt, and regret as a way of self-punishment. I have ministered to many people who cannot forgive themselves. When they don't forgive themselves, it is a way of punishing themselves for the sin they committed against loved ones. I've known numerous people who committed adultery, and not forgiving themselves is a form of self-punishment for sinning against their spouses. It is a way to punish themselves since their spouses don't know. It is a reminder not to sin again.

The good news is that Christ took our punishment upon Himself so we can live in freedom and victory. We can't live in something we don't have, and when we are keeping ourselves in bondage, we are keeping ourselves shackled and chained to our past mistakes. Christ died so we may have life. We can live the life He intended for us and be fruitful for the kingdom of God when the shackles and chains of the past have been released.

Forgiving ourselves is the hardest thing to do, but it must be done. Instead of beating yourself up repeatedly for your mistakes, ask the Holy Spirit to help you move through your regrets and sin. Ask Him to help you remove self-condemnation and walk in the freedom and victory that Jesus Christ purchased for you. If you continually badger yourself about past mistakes, you live in defeat instead of being the overcomer and conqueror Christ says you can be. My book *Unshackled* shares more on forgiveness. (See the appendix.)

Prophetic Exercise: Forgive Yourself and Others

Write down and meditate with the Holy Spirit's assistance:

- Do you need to extend forgiveness to anyone? Who?
- What do you need to break agreement with, including specific actions, words, sin, guilt, shame, regret, and self-condemnation?
- List any sins you need to forgive yourself for committing.

Abolish Word Curses

There is power in word curses spoken over and about us, including words we have released out of our own mouths. Proverbs 18:21 tells us, "Death and life are in the power of the tongue, and those who love it will eat its fruit." Whether we have spoken the words or someone else has, spoken word curses are powerful in the spiritual realm. To break these curses, we must remove demonic access, repent, forgive, and seek forgiveness. Our attempt in this chapter is to remove demonic access points. We don't want the enemy to be able to find us guilty of anything. We want to be acquitted of all charges. And to be acquitted, we need to rescind what has been spoken forth in the spiritual atmosphere.

When people speak negatively about us, it puts forth word curses in the spiritual atmosphere. The demonic realm can ignite and activate those word curses. They can block our prophecies and prevent our freedom. Word curses take flight in the spiritual atmosphere to activate demonic attacks. Satan is "the prince of the power of the air" (Eph. 2:2). The demonic realm can be activated from words that go up into the spiritual atmosphere. Demons are waiting to activate spoken words.

When negative words are spoken, they can prevent our destinies and block our prophecies. There is a saying, "We become who we surround ourselves with." We can take on a mentality of victimhood or defeat and feel condemned about what people say about us. Feeling lowly and defeated can prevent us from pressing through to our breakthroughs or believing God will move in our lives as He said He would.

When you hear negativity about yourself long enough, you start to believe it, and it attacks the very core of your being.

As spiritual attacks occur, your prophecies are delayed from manifestation, and as you experience victim and defeat mentality, you don't receive the freedom Christ intended.

People with whom you have disagreements can throw insults and injury toward you. They may have no idea that the enemy uses these words to deter your destiny. When word curses of offense, anger, bitterness, and slander activate, they ignite an all-out war in the demonic realm over your future.

We often don't credit these words as spiritual igniters, but they are dangerous weapons the devil uses to counterattack the will of God for our lives. When we don't clean up the spiritual atmosphere and annihilate these forces against us, unseen warfare happens in the spiritual realm that manifests in the natural realm.

Prophetic Exercise: Prayer to Rescind Word Curses

Praying on the offense is necessary to keep a clear and clean atmosphere around you. If you have never prayed against word curses over and about you, I suggest you pray defensively now and counterattack the enemy's measures against you.

> I bind and rebuke every word curse spoken over and about me. I command all negative activations in the spirit realm to be destroyed and burned up by the fire of God. I speak and decree every word curse that has dispatched against me, my destiny, my finances, and my health to be severed in Jesus' name. I proclaim that every word curse through gossip and slander be abolished in the spiritual realm. In the name of Jesus I rebuke all word curses spoken about me.

RESCIND SELF-INVITED WORD CURSES

We can curse ourselves by what we speak out. Simple words such as "That makes me sick," "You're going to kill me for this," or "She drives me crazy" are all word curses that give the devil a legal right. I remember sitting in a conference once, and the presenter was talking about a spirit of death. He specifically went into word curses and what we say, things such as "You're killing me," "I'm going to kill you for that," or "You're going to die laughing when you hear this." He continued to teach and then rebuked and took authority over the spirit of death. He prayed and said over the audience, "Spirit of death, I command you to get out and go, in Jesus' name." He prayed for a couple of minutes and kept ordering the demonic spirits to leave.

I felt three demonic spirits of death leave my body that instant. A part of me couldn't believe a tongues-talking, Spirit-filled Christian had cursed herself and invited spirits of death into her life. But I couldn't deny what I felt as those demons manifested out of my body. I knew as they left that I had invited them in because I was one of those people who would say words such as *kill*, *die*, or *death* jokingly and in casual conversations.

Our words have so much power that whether we are walking in dominion, declaring them forth, or speaking them in casual conversation, we will experience the materialization of them. We must repent, renounce, and rescind the effects of these words over our lives. (We'll do this in the prophetic activation section below.)

It's Time for Activation

Let's renounce the legal rights we've given to the enemy of our souls.

Prayer of Repentance, Renunciation, and Breaking Agreement

Heavenly Father, I repent of all ungodly and unholy actions. I sever and break ties with all sin and word curses expelled from my mouth. I come against any dark power attempting to infiltrate my ground and plant demonic seeds in my life. I bind and restrict the enemy from having demonic access in my life. I break agreement with unforgiveness, word curses, and every destructive habit in my life. I renounce sin in my life, emotional ailments that have become strongholds, and places that I have not edified and glorified Your name. I break agreement with demonic powers that I have enabled due to my inactivity and disobedience. I ask for Your forgiveness, and I choose this day to forgive myself. I forgive myself for all sin, mistakes, past failures, times I have hurt and abused others, and everything I have done that has released darkness and cursing instead of light and love. Fill me, Holy Spirit, with Your overwhelming love, peace, and goodness. I pray this in the name of Jesus Christ, the Messiah. Amen!

Impartation and Activation Prayer

Holy Spirit, please give me a heart of forgiveness and repentance. I receive Your love and ask You to fill me overwhelmingly with Your love so that I can extend it to others. Help me be a vessel of Your love. I ask You, Holy Spirit, to help me exude the fruit of the Spirit at all times. Fill me with love, joy, peace, patience, gentleness, goodness, faith, meekness, and self-control.

Prophetic Proclamations (Faith Declarations)

I proclaim I am walking by faith and not by sight! I am an overcomer! I overcome offenses against me, and I forgive quickly.

I am forgiven; therefore, releasing forgiveness is a natural reaction to who I am since the Spirit of the Lord lives inside me.

I receive the overwhelming love of the Father to help me walk in strength, hope, integrity, and peace. He is my overwhelming substance and the source of power I draw from.

I submit to the will of the Father for my life. Father God, use me to impact people with Your love and forgiveness.

I glorify the Lord in words and actions. I declare that everything I do brings glory and honor to His name!

Spiritual Activation

1. Develop a technique in which you choose to forgive. For example, when unforgiveness or offense tries to attack my mind, I imagine it running off my shoulder and down my arm. I don't allow it to come into my mind and take root.
2. Speak out and declare over different situations in your life as appropriate, "I forgive myself." Keep speaking it until you feel an emotional release, tears, or peace.
3. Rebuke word curses you may have released into the spiritual atmosphere. Speak and declare audibly, "Every word curse, idle word, and negative word I have spoken, I rebuke and rescind. I command that they will not affect my life or the person I spoke them about. In Jesus' name I cancel every demonic deployment and assignment that has activated as a result of my words."

Spiritual Warfare Declarations

Pray on the offense, not the defense. Protect yourself in the natural and spiritual by speaking out warfare prayers and declarations to bind and restrict every evil force against you.

In the name of Jesus I confine and restrict every demonic deployment against my destiny.

I speak and declare no root of unforgiveness or offense will implant within my soul. I command spirits of infirmity from unforgiveness to get out in Jesus' name.

I command the spirit of offense to be bound and restricted immediately upon deployment. You will not enter my mind or heart. I will not allow you a foothold in my life.

I annihilate every dark power that would cause division, strife, and dissension in my relationships. I speak protection over my relationships.

I rebuke every spirit of unforgiveness sent on assignment against my mind and emotions. In Jesus' name I command you will not complete your mission.

Chapter 14

JESUS' PASSION FOR DELIVERANCE

SALVATION ISN'T A get-out-of-jail-free card. When we accept Christ into our hearts, most of us do it because the gospel has been enticingly presented to us, and we desire to come and know the Jesus someone intimately told us about. When we talk about salvation and repenting and giving our lives over to Christ, people are in a hurry to tell you about the one-way ticket to heaven you can obtain. But they don't go into detail about the full atonement of the cross now available to you.

When I was saved, the biggest push I received from other Christians was getting me to pray in tongues. I felt so much pressure to receive my prayer language. Not once did anyone tell me about Jesus being Healer and Deliverer. I've lived with the Lord in my heart for thirty-three years. I got sick like everyone else and had demonic bondage for years. Suppose these same people who were enthusiastic about my getting my prayer language had been as eager to tell me about healing and deliverance. In that case, I could have lived a lot more of those thirty-three years in victory instead of defeat.

I believe accepting Christ into our hearts and getting people saved is a good thing, but we can't stop there. We evangelize in elevators, malls, and restaurants. We tell people about Jesus on street corners and anywhere else the Spirit of the Lord leads us. But then what's next?

I always bring my Be Love cards with me when I evangelize. These are business-card-sized cards that I have custom printed to say, "You were loved on today by a Kathy DeGraw Ministries team member." The cards provide our contact information if they need additional prayer, a church to attend, or someone to minister to them. I do this because Jesus instructed us to make disciples, not to lead them to Christ and leave them.

The finished work of the cross is about repenting (which is more than saying you're sorry; it requires changing direction, turning away from your old life, and giving your entire heart to Jesus) and desiring to serve God and people. It is advancing the kingdom of God, loving God and people, and serving God and people. However, when Jesus went to the cross, He died for our physical healing and deliverance too. When we lead people to salvation through Jesus, we often fail to introduce the other important elements people need as they begin their walks with Christ. I believe there should be a progression of salvation, water baptism, deliverance ministry, and plugging into a good Spirit-filled church, small group, or Bible study. People need the complete package of coming into a relationship with Jesus Christ, not just a get-out-of-hell-free card.

I remember when my husband was pastoring and his district superintendent told him he could preach about grace but not about demons. My husband responded with, "Then I'd only be preaching half of the Gospels." Jesus died to forgive our sins, but He also came to liberate those who are oppressed. If we tell people about salvation but fall short on the rest, we are only preaching half of the Bible. People are interested in going to heaven, but they are also looking for solutions to their problems. They desire to be healed and not have to worry about physical disease. They want to change, but they don't realize they have been plagued with rejection, abandonment, and unworthiness. Therefore, when we lead them to the Savior, we must also lead them to and through the solution.

Jesus Was All In

Jesus came for more than salvation, as we see when He quoted Isaiah.

> The Spirit of the Lord is upon Me, because He has anointed Me to preach the gospel to the poor; He has sent Me to heal the broken-hearted, to preach deliverance to the captives and recovery of sight to the blind, to set at liberty those who are oppressed; to preach the acceptable year of the Lord.
>
> —Luke 4:18–19

Jesus not only preached, but He ministered. I love that Jesus put all of Himself into ministering. We can see that when He cleansed the leper.

> So He preached in their synagogues throughout Galilee and cast out demons. A leper came to Him, pleading with Him and kneeling before Him, saying, "If You are willing, You can make me clean."
>
> Then Jesus, moved with compassion, extended His hand and touched him, and said to him, "I will. Be clean." As soon as He had spoken, the leprosy immediately departed from him, and he was cleansed.
>
> —Mark 1:39–42

Jesus invested Himself emotionally, physically, and spiritually. He was moved with compassion, extended His hand, and was willing to make the man with leprosy clean and whole. Jesus touched this man with every part of His being because setting the oppressed free and healing the sick was important to Jesus.

However, Jesus was so passionate about putting His entire self into releasing the kingdom that He also took the disciples along and taught them how to minister. Jesus did the five most important things in ministry. He discipled, preached, taught, healed, and delivered, and He did it all in love and compassion. The purpose of the cross did not end with eternal life with Jesus in heaven. He wants us to walk in complete victory—body, mind, and soul! He came so we could have life and have it abundantly (John 10:10)—now, here on earth! We don't have to wait until we get to heaven to live abundantly, be overcomers, and have victory. It all belongs to us now.

The Atonement

Isaiah breaks down what Jesus provided at the cross and the grueling death He went through to accomplish it.

> Surely he has borne our grief and carried our sorrows; yet we esteemed him stricken, smitten of God, and afflicted. But he was wounded for our transgressions, he was bruised for our iniquities; the chastisement of our peace was upon him, and by his stripes we are healed. All of us like sheep have gone astray; each of us has turned to his own way, but the Lord has laid on him the iniquity of us all. He was oppressed, and he was afflicted, yet he opened not his mouth;

> he was brought as a lamb to the slaughter, and as a sheep before its shearers is silent, so he opened not his mouth.
>
> —Isaiah 53:4–7

I am amazed every time I study Isaiah 53. I am completely undone by what Jesus endured for us. He came down from heaven and had none of His glory. He became a child and then a man to endure suffering for us. He was continually despised and rejected. People outright avoided Him. They turned their faces from Him.

This scripture describes Him as a man of disease. Could you think about that? He was a man of disease. Even though we couldn't see physical disease on Him, He carried our physical illnesses to the cross. Think about how we handle being around people who are physically sick and contagious. If they cough or sneeze, we run the other way. Yes, Jesus, despised and rejected by men, took on our disease, touched a leper, and was not hesitant to touch and get near those we would consider victimized or contagious.

We can take this a step further. Some people are extremely sensitive to the spiritual realm and can sense when people are demonically oppressed. It might be tempting to run from these situations, not wanting to feel the oppression of others. However, if you have this spiritual gift, I pray you will run to them, desiring to help them and set them free. Jesus was the perfect example of getting His entire being involved in liberation of the captives.

He was a man of disease, taking on our sickness and experiencing our grief. Our infirmities and our emotional bondage were lifted off us, put on Him, and taken to the cross. When we carry burdens, worry, and fear, we aren't fully receiving the finished work of the cross. Why do we own, claim, focus, and talk about something that has been taken off us? Sometimes we think and speak more about our conditions or medical diagnoses than our belief that Jesus can heal us. Instead of seeing ourselves as fleshly beings with imperfect bodies that suffer from infirmities and afflictions, we need to see ourselves as spiritual beings, perfected and made in His image. He suffered for us so we wouldn't have to suffer.

Prophetic Exercise: Prayer for Healing

Declare a prayer like the following, and begin to receive your healing now!

> Sickness and disease, I command you to leave my body and evacuate the premises. I speak and decree to my body to come into alignment with the Word of God. I declare by His wounds and stripes I am healed. I am not a victim; I am victorious. I receive the finished work of the cross with all victory. I am not defeated. In the name of Jesus I command every medical diagnosis to be reversed and every evil perpetrator invading my soul to be evicted and eradicated. I decree complete freedom, healing, and deliverance, and I receive the atonement of the cross in its fullness. I speak and decree I am physically and emotionally healed and made whole. I command my body and mind to be fully restored and strengthened. In Jesus' name I declare I am healed and delivered, and I receive my full healing and deliverance.

Jesus purchased our deliverance, but we often hop from ministry to ministry, trying to receive that deliverance from a man or woman who is anointed to cast out demons instead of receiving deliverance from Jesus. But when we idolize men and women, we will never see our deliverance manifest. He was wounded for our crimes, sins, and rebellion. He was disciplined for us.

Our demonic bondage is not only because of generational curses, trauma, or soul ties. Most of our demonic bondage is our own fault. We took in the hurt, pain, offense, and rejection. We allowed emotions to grow into more than what they should have. Pride invaded our souls, control became a way of life, and fear inhibited us. Jesus purchased these very things that we are spending years trying to release. If we would focus on receiving what He purchased and His love, we wouldn't have to work hard to obtain our deliverance. He was disciplined for us, but some of us punish ourselves by not giving up what He already took to the cross.

Studying Isaiah 53, we can see a complete package of healing and deliverance. This was the accomplished work of the cross. Why are we not receiving what He already accomplished and manifested? Repent for not receiving it. Declare out right now!

Prophetic Exercise:
Prayer of Repentance

Jesus, I repent. Forgive me! I'm sorry for not receiving the manifested work of the cross. I rid myself of defeat and victim mentality. I repent for lack of knowledge and understanding. I break agreement with every demonic power, my flesh, and any thoughts and actions keeping me in bondage. Jesus, You came to be my bondage breaker. I receive. Help me to release it all to You. I declare there is no place for strongholds in a kingdom citizen, and I am a kingdom citizen. Therefore worry, fear, lack, passivity, distrust, and everything else must go now in Jesus' name!

All of our iniquity was laid on Jesus at once. There is instant deliverance and freedom when we receive this message. There are times we need to work out our deliverance, but there is also supernatural freedom available when we receive the message in the Bible. Part of our deliverance is receiving what He already has done for us. The Word is prophetic, and when we read the Word, deliverance can and does manifest because the Bible is a big book of freedom. Mind transitions and a complete understanding of what He did will help us to capture the deliverance He purchased and break free from the chains that hold us back from our full potential. This is the truth of God's Word; therefore let's receive some deliverance right now!

Prophetic Exercise:
Prayer of Deliverance

Holy Spirit, I receive the truth of Your Word, and right now I receive deliverance. I declare complete freedom in my mind, body, and soul. My identity is in Christ, and I accept what the Word says about me. I trust You, Jesus, for my deliverance. I speak to every demonic entity keeping me in bondage, and I eradicate you from my soul by the blood of Jesus! I declare that every blueprint of hell established against me is burned up by the fire of God. I restrict demonic powers from carrying out assignments against my destiny. Rejection, fear, unworthiness, and control, I destroy you and the stronghold you have had on my life. Intimidation, I command you to release me and enter me no more. I receive the truth of God's Word that Jesus died for my sins, healing, deliverance, and strongholds. I bind and restrict every strongman in my life, and I tell you to go and get out in Jesus' name. I declare whom the Son sets free is free indeed, and I thank You, Lord. You set me free, and I am free indeed. I speak and declare by Christ's stripes I am healed and delivered, and my mind is freed from every stronghold and mind-binding spirit. I abolish every sin and demonic attack in my life, in the precious name of Jesus, my Messiah. Amen!

I can hardly get past the next verse I am going to write about. It moves me every time. "He was oppressed, and he was afflicted, yet he opened not his mouth; he was brought as a lamb to the slaughter, and as a sheep before its shearers is silent, so he opened not his mouth" (Isa. 53:7). He was mistreated, took our punishment, and never complained. He did not open His mouth.

One word and He could have saved Himself, but He chose to endure for us. WOW! What perseverance to the end! He submitted. He took our beatings. He could have dispatched angels on assignment, but He didn't. He was led as a sheep to the slaughter. He sacrificed His body for your healing and deliverance. He didn't open His mouth. He kept silent.

When we don't receive atonement, healing, and deliverance, in essence we are saying that nothing Jesus did mattered because we didn't receive it. I hate that thought. He persevered when He could have quit. Receiving what He did makes His sacrifice worth it and honorable. I don't want my life to say His sacrifice didn't matter. It does matter. I feel the emotion of this as I write it. My heart is grieved, not condemned, for the times I don't do it right. I think we need to all remember Jesus' sacrifice on a more regular basis.

Jesus suffered so many injustices. He was arrested, taken away, and people were yelling, "Crucify Him!" His followers weren't protesting; they were keeping silent. Some were even encouraging these events. I can't imagine how He felt, yet He persisted.

When I think of what He suffered, I think of the movie *The Passion of the Christ*. The scene that gets to me is when Jesus is at the whipping post. He's down on His knees from the pain and agony of being beaten. John, Mary, and Mary walk into the courtyard. Jesus sees them and stands back up for more beatings. I am not saying this scene in the movie is accurate, but I love what it conveys—that Jesus knew what He had to do, and in those moments when He felt He couldn't go on, it was His great love for us that motivated Him to see it through. He had done no violence, no deceit was in His mouth, but He took the punishment. How many times are deceit, gossip, slander, betrayal, and offense in our mouths?

And again, this verse gets me every time. "Yet it pleased the LORD to bruise him; He has put him to grief. If he made himself as an offering for sin, he shall see his offspring, he shall prolong his days, and the good pleasure of the LORD shall prosper in his hand" (Isa. 53:10). It pleased Adonai to crush Jesus with illness and our emotional pain. It pleased the Father to crush His Son. Oh my! This isn't easy to comprehend in the natural. It pleased Adonai to make His Son suffer, to make Him an offering for our sin. It isn't just a one-way ticket to heaven. He died for our healing and deliverance.

Our Father offered up His only Son for us. It is the resurrected redemption power of the cross. It didn't stop at the cross. He was resurrected, and now that resurrection power lives in you! Therefore tell your sickness and disease to go. The same power that raised Christ from the dead lives in you!

Prophetic Exercise: Prayer to Receive Healing and Deliverance

Command any sickness or disease attacking your body to go now in the name of Jesus! Evict every evil spirit from your soul and body! Receive your healing!

> Sickness and disease must go! Get out of me in Jesus' name! I break agreement with physical afflictions. In the name of Jesus I command spirits of infirmity to leave my body and creative miracles to come forth! I speak to my body, and I say, be restored and healed in Jesus' name! I command health and healing to come forth.

Speak this out until you feel that spirit leave. Speak to it until you feel a shift in the atmosphere and something moves or happens.

> I command every demonic perpetrator to leave now in Jesus' name. I break agreement with passivity! I break agreement with fear! I break agreement with demonic oppression! I break agreement with rejection! I break agreement with every evil spirit attacking my soul. I say that the spiritual realm is shifting on my behalf. Divine intervention is coming forth! Deliverance is manifesting! I receive my liberation! My freedom day is here! I believe and receive in Jesus' name.

Keep going and relying on the Holy Spirit to bubble up and give you drops of what needs to be prayed and spoken out.

> I command, I decree, and I establish permanent renewal, good things, prosperous things, healings, deliverance, miracles, and discernment increase. I thank You, Lord Jesus, that by Your stripes I am healed. I'm not looking for my healing. I'm walking in my healing. Body, manifest

change! Mind, be renewed! Demons, you have no hold on me! I seal it in and pray it all in Jesus' name.

Continue to speak it out! Keep going! You got it! Declare it! Own it! Possess what is yours! Decree a change.

JESUS MINISTERED HEALING AND DELIVERANCE

Not only did Jesus purchase our healing and deliverance at the cross, but when He was here on earth, He liberated people emotionally and physically when He ministered. Sickness can be related to a spiritual stronghold. When we seek healing, we also need to explore the option of a demonic stronghold or generational curse attached to the sickness.

When we study the Gospels, we find that Jesus ministered healing and deliverance together.

> His fame went throughout all Syria. And they brought to Him all sick people who were taken with various diseases and tormented with pain, those who were possessed with demons, those who had seizures, and those who had paralysis, and He healed them.
>
> —MATTHEW 4:24

> A centurion came to Him, entreating Him, and saying, "Lord, my servant is lying at home, sick with paralysis, terribly tormented."
>
> Jesus said to him, "I will come and heal him."
>
> The centurion answered and said, "Lord, I am not worthy that You should come under my roof. But speak the word only, and my servant will be healed."
>
> —MATTHEW 8:5–8

> When the evening came, they brought to Him many who were possessed with demons. And He cast out the spirits with His word, and healed all who were sick.
>
> —Matthew 8:16

> In the evening, when the sun had set, they brought to Him all who were sick and those who were possessed with demons.
>
> —Mark 1:32

> So they went out and preached that men should repent. And they cast out many demons and anointed with oil many who were sick and healed them.
>
> —Mark 6:12–13

In the Great Commission, Jesus mentioned healing and deliverance together.

> He said to them, "Go into all the world, and preach the gospel to every creature. He who believes and is baptized will be saved. But he who does not believe will be condemned. These signs will accompany those who believe: In My name they will cast out demons; they will speak with new tongues; they will take up serpents; if they drink any deadly thing, it will not hurt them; they will lay hands on the sick, and they will recover."
>
> —Mark 16:15–18

I have always thought it was interesting that the first thing He instructed us to do is cast out demons. It was also the first ministry He exuded with His disciples. Yet so many leave out the very ministry Jesus commanded us to do. We can't have a healing ministry without deliverance. As we study the life of Jesus, healing and deliverance go together. And if we are to be like Jesus—and we are—then we must release this ministry together as He did.

IT'S TIME FOR ACTIVATION

Let's pray to receive everything Jesus died for—forgiveness, healing, and deliverance.

PRAYER OF REPENTANCE, RENUNCIATION, AND BREAKING AGREEMENT

I repent of lack of knowledge and any place I have been legalistic or ignorant in my thinking. I renounce any false teaching and idleness I have had when believing in healing and deliverance. I repent of not allowing the Holy Spirit to prophetically speak to me about the Scriptures and convict me of truth. I break agreement with fleshly tendencies and thinking. I repent for not leaving room to be taught more from the Holy Spirit. I speak and decree I am teachable. I cast down all pride in Jesus' name.

IMPARTATION AND ACTIVATION PRAYER

Jesus, I receive the full atonement of the cross. I thank You for dying for my sins so that I could be forgiven and live with You in heaven. I repent of sin. I break agreement with sin, addictions, trauma, and wrong actions and motives. Jesus, I ask You to come into my heart. I desire to change and live my life for You. I believe in the full atonement of the cross. I receive the healing and deliverance You purchased for me. Help me to serve You and be kingdom oriented. In Jesus' name, amen!

Prophetic Proclamations (Faith Declarations)

I receive physical healing in my body. Body, I command you to line up to the Word of God and come into complete health.

I believe and receive inner healing and deliverance into my soul. I command that my mind, will, and emotions are coming into freedom and that I will press in to receive my deliverance.

I believe healing and deliverance go together, and I will pursue knowledge and manifestation of both of these in my life.

I live my life for Jesus and the glorification and edification of His name.

I exalt the Lord with my words, actions, and life. Lord, my life is Yours. I completely surrender to You.

Spiritual Activation

1. Activate your healing. Where do you need to receive healing? Read healing scriptures, write a declaration, and begin to believe in the full manifestation of your healing.

2. Activate your deliverance. What strongholds have been resisting eviction in your life? Break agreement with strongholds. Say and speak out loud, "I break agreement with the stronghold of [insert name], and I command you to leave in Jesus' name."
3. Cast out demons. As you pray for people and command healing to come forth, cast out the correlating demonic spirits attacking them and making them sick.

Spiritual Warfare Declarations

I command every demonic spirit that has been slumbering and dormant inside me to release me and leave now in Jesus' name.

I bind and restrict demons from entering my soul due to sin. When I sin, I quickly repent and leave no open door to the enemy. I cancel and nullify demonic strategies against me.

I vanquish every attack of the enemy. I declare that I am an overcomer and evil spirits cannot torment me.

In the name of Jesus I command any sickness or disease attempting to invade my body to leave now, and any medical diagnosis or condition that attempts to manifest in my body to cease your assignment now.

In Jesus' name I call off every evil spirit of affliction against my life. I am an overcomer and victorious!

Chapter 15

PROPHETIC ACTIVATION

Allow me to share a little more about that season in my life when I felt the Lord leading me to operate in the prophetic. As I wrote earlier, I would partner with the Holy Spirit when it came to operating in most of the gifts of the Spirit, but when it came to releasing the prophetic, I held back because I had seen the prophetic misused. People would go to a prophetic person for a word instead of going to prayer and increasing their relationships with the Lord to hear from Him. They wanted the easy way out—for someone to speak to them instead of investing and spending time with the Lord.

The Lord was trying to get my attention and activate the prophetic call inside of me. He instructed me through my prayer time to take a ministry trip out of town with my team. Now that may seem normal for a person in ministry, but I had to rely on the Holy Spirit for every move. He revealed the location—a city and state—in which we were to proceed. As we approached the city, we had to partner with the Holy Spirit for where to go and what to do. We didn't know His intentions for us. I first heard Him say, "Go up," and He brought me to a verse in Deuteronomy. We looked for buildings in which we could go up and see over the city. He would give us different directions to follow, such as, "Go to this church," "Find a round building" (yes, there was a round building), "Drive along the waterfront," and other instructions. As we followed His directions, it would lead us to more revelation, we would meet people to pray for, or we would pray for that region. We went for forty-eight hours entirely led on guidance from the Holy Spirit, including where to get gas, eat, and sleep.

Through His instructions during this trip, the Spirit led us to connect with a local pastor who ended up being a prophetic apostle. The apostle asked me whether I was prophetic, and I replied, "Yes." But he didn't know that I was just beginning to prophesy and hadn't fully embraced my prophetic calling. He invited me to his church the next day to prophesy over his congregation. I had never prophesied over an entire assembly before. But I knew through prayer, discernment, and the series of events the Holy Spirit led us through that the Lord had brought me to this church, so I went forth with faith.

I ended up prophesying over about seventy people, and he called me the next day and told me everything I said was accurate. However, he didn't stop there. He stretched me and said, "Let's call a couple of prophets and encourage them." These prophets had been walking in the office of prophet for forty years, and to be honest, I thought, "Who am I to be prophesying to the prophets of old?" I was only forty years old and prophesying to prophets who had been in ministry as long as I had been alive. Nevertheless he called them, and I prophesied. I was shaking in my boots, but both prophecies were accurate, and the prophets were blessed. They even called me back when one word manifested in three days.

I was out of my comfort zone, but I had to be pushed. I would have delayed the prophetic call on my life even longer if it weren't for being stretched. I needed what I call prophetic boot camp. The Lord verified what I was experiencing through Scripture, prophetic actions, and books and songs what He was doing in that season of my life to activate the prophetic. Some people think that the prophetic should simply flow out, that it is a gift to be supernaturally released, and while that can be true, sometimes the gift needs to be activated. Timothy even told us to stir up the gift within us. (See 2 Timothy 1:6.)

Jesus told us to make disciples. (See Matthew 28:19.) Discipleship comes from someone walking alongside us to assist us in releasing the gifts God has given us. I like to describe it as doing life together and getting a spiritual boot kick to get you going. There are times when we need to be pushed and propelled to the next place in our spiritual walks. Insecurity and intimidation are two culprits that stifle us in our giftings and make us hesitant to step out.

When we have prophetic oversight, mentoring, and encouragement, it stretches us to step out and release what God has anointed us to do. I like to take people by my side and bring out their giftings. When I am training a team member or intern, the Holy Spirit will often tell me they have a prophetic word to release. I will tell them, and half the time, they were pondering something but were hesitant to release it in fear of being wrong. Other times they had no idea there was something in them. However, as they stop, pray, and partner with the Holy Spirit, something arises, and they are quickened to discern.

Just as we need to partner with the Holy Spirit, sometimes we need to partner with a person who has been there before and can help push something out of us. Until you know and can hear the Holy Spirit's voice clearly and confidently, He may use a prophetic person to pull out of you what He put on the inside of you! The kingdom of God is within you!

Everything you need is inside you! You need to release it! Confidence and boldness are not something everyone has. Therefore, having someone believe in you and what the Spirit of the Lord has placed in you is beneficial—both for you and for the person receiving what you have to give. As I wrote earlier, Jesus has called us to make disciples, and part of that is equipping and activating people, showing them how to move in the Spirit, and even allowing them to make mistakes.

This book was written so you could be activated. My goal has been to propel and release your destiny, stir your gifts, and give you the confidence and boldness to speak out and step out. In each chapter's closing prophetic activation section, I have released spiritual exercises and decrees led by the Holy Spirit.

I want the Holy Spirit to teach you the same way He has taught me. Years ago I learned to trust and rely on the Holy Spirit as my best friend. I learned to take a step back, breathe, and allow Him to lead me in ministering to people. I don't want to speak or act out unless He instructs me.

I know you, too, desire the Holy Spirit's direction, wisdom, instruction, and impartation. The idea behind these exercises and practical applications was to train you to rely on Him and trust that He will speak to you and guide you too! For me it took a two-year journey, facedown on the carpet before the Lord, to get to know the Father, Son, and Holy Spirit. What will your journey look like? The Holy Spirit can be your most reliable friend. If you skipped the activations at the end of each chapter as you read this book, I want to encourage you to go back and do each prophetic activation. They will take you beyond knowledge to application.

You have a destiny that only you can fulfill, and you need to complete your destiny. God needs you to achieve your destiny, and the people you will influence need you to fulfill your destiny.

It's Time for Activation

Let's do a final activation session together. Additionally I want to invite you to check out my e-courses at kathydegrawministries.org to further activate you in the prophetic, spiritual warfare, and deliverance.

Prayer of Repentance, Renunciation, and Breaking Agreement

A spiritual shift occurs and freedom manifests when we pray audibly. Speaking out causes our faith to increase, and when evil spirits hear our declarations, their activity must cease as we exude our authority. Speak this prayer declaration out loud:

> *I repent and renounce of all false teaching, legalism, and religious beliefs and practices that do not align with the Word of God. I repent of any false ideas and wrong mindsets I had about the kingdom of God, demonic entities, or spiritual warfare. I break agreement with strongholds that have inhibited me and with my fleshly thoughts and tendencies. I submit my soul and my flesh to the Holy Spirit. I ask the Holy Spirit to come in and convict and correct me. I renounce every word that did not edify that I spoke out into the spirit realm from my lack of knowledge and enthusiasm for the things of the Lord. I rebuke, renounce, and repent of any and all ungodly activities and places I acted out in my flesh due*

to woundedness. I speak and decree that I am set free by the blood of Jesus, and I receive fully the reconciliation paid for me by Jesus at the cross. In Jesus' name, amen!

Prophetic Action to Activation

Our words are prophetically assigned and get spiritual results. When we prophesy and declare into the spiritual atmosphere, we create a divine shift in our circumstances. Our faith is activated by believing and hearing what we just released into the atmosphere. Speaking out our faith and prophetic decrees is a way to release and activate the prophetic within us. The devil hates it when we speak out faith. By speaking out, we are doing what I call homework. Evil spirits monitor our activities, and they know when we are praying and speaking faith versus fear. They can keep you in stagnancy because they have a legal right to do so when you are not being a warrior. Speaking out prophetic proclamations is prophesying over yourself what you want to happen. Change your circumstances by praying the impartation and activation prayer audibly. The prophetic proclamations and faith declarations in each chapter can easily be bookmarked for easy reference to pray out regularly.

Impartation and Activation Prayer

Pray this prayer audibly with a heart and mind to receive what is being released from heaven.

Heavenly Father, thank You for sending the Holy Spirit. I receive this teaching and willingly apply it to my life. Help me to walk in the Spirit. I

> *thank You for a renewed spirit. I thank You for fresh impartation and activation. I invite You in, Holy Spirit. Holy Spirit, use me! Partner with me! I want more of You! I raise my expectations for the manifestation of the Spirit in my life. I activate the prophetic within me through Your Spirit. Guide me to continue to increase and release. I thank You, Holy Spirit, for Your love for me.*

Prophetic Proclamations (Faith Declarations)

Prophesy over yourself and increase your faith by releasing these prophetic proclamations audibly into the spiritual atmosphere.

> I prophesy and speak into existence that I will activate the prophetic inside of me. I willingly partner with the Holy Spirit in everything I do.
>
> I release prophetic words fluently and accurately. I rely on the Holy Spirit to give me words of wisdom, words of knowledge, and prophetic words to speak out and edify, encourage, and exhort others.
>
> I wage warfare in the spiritual realm from the finished work of the cross, knowing that Jesus accomplished it all for me. I partner with the Holy Spirit when I need to pray and declare to bind and restrict demonic forces or proclaim and call forth blessings from heaven.
>
> I speak and my words are prophetically assigned and targeted to hit a result. I expect a spiritual shift when I speak out. I proclaim that what I speak in the natural

must manifest in the natural and spiritual. I seek the Holy Spirit for the prophetic unction to speak according to the will of God and word of God.

I declare I will allow the Holy Spirit to guide me in my day-to-day operations. I will seek the Holy Spirit before making decisions in the natural. I will be obedient and disciplined to the Spirit's instructions and convictions.

Holy Spirit, come upon me now in might and power! Holy Spirit, fill me to overflowing!

Spiritual Activation

Activation can come in the natural or supernatural. When we practice what we learn, we can increase the acceleration of what we received. Our faith grows as we implement what we learned. Activate what you learned by practicing the three spiritual warfare exercises. The exercises don't have to be completed all at once. I suggest you try one for a while and then move to the next one. Try the activation with some friends, a small group, or in your meditative time.

1. Practice engaging in warfare prophetically led by the Spirit. Think of a situation you are experiencing that needs supernatural breakthrough. Enter into the presence of God, and wait for the Holy Spirit to reveal to you the prayer strategy to get your breakthrough.
2. Seek the Holy Spirit for instructions for your life and ministry for the next year. Spend time in prayer, fasting, solitude, and rest in His presence. Write down what He speaks to you.

Expect Him to reveal what direction He wants you to take and how to get there.

3. Increase your spiritual senses and discernment by having a strong devotional time and practice. Be diligent to make worship, Bible study, and prayer a part of your daily routine. Staying in a place of love and His presence comes from being with Him. Sometimes we don't hear from the Holy Spirit because we haven't been with Him to hear from Him.

Spiritual Warfare Declarations

Pray on the offense, not just the defense. Protect yourself in the natural and spiritual by speaking out warfare prayers and declarations to bind and restrict every evil force against you. Living a life partnering with the Holy Spirit in prayer will help you conquer warfare attacks. Praying out intense warfare declarations with authority and power and knowing your identity in Christ will pack a powerful punch in the spirit realm. Get up and get moving in your prayer time. Praying on your feet, if you can, will help to intensify your prayer life and get you involved emotionally, spiritually, and physically. Repeat the declarations three times each until you gain strength and authority. Each time you pray them out, you should feel a more intense prayer arise. After you get comfortable praying these prayers, I encourage you to write your own warfare prayers against your situation. My book *SPEAK OUT* will teach you how to write warfare prayers based on natural knowledge, prophetic insights, or Scripture. (See the appendix.)

In the name of Jesus I annihilate and apprehend in the

spirit every dark force coming against my destiny.

I rebuke the devourer, and I tell you to get your hands off my blessings. I call forth my increase. I call forth prophetic revelation to receive financial abundance. I proclaim creative and strategic ideas are coming my way, and I bind and rebuke demonic forces from coming against my successes and victories.

I take authority over every evil spirit in my generational line, every familiar and territorial spirit, and every spirit trying to come against my ministry, career, and business. I say patterns, cycles, and seasons of the past will not be reiterated. I apply the blood of Christ to everything I put my hands to.

I command the spirit of death and destruction over my health and body to go now in Jesus' name. I decree that my healing is manifesting because of what Jesus did for me. Body, be whole! Sickness, leave! Demonic attacks against my health, be destroyed now by the blood of Jesus.

I speak and decree that every evil spirit that has plagued me for years leaves now! You have been served eviction-notice papers! Get out! I call off your deployments! I say I am blessed!

Mind-binding spirits that have tormented me and caused trauma in my life, cease to exist in Jesus' name. Desist from your assignment. I command my mind to not be plagued with fear, anxiety, stress, worry, or depression. I speak and decree that I am free from the battlefield in my mind and that I have victory over all things in the name of Jesus. Amen.

CLOSING PROPHETIC WORD

YOUR LIFE IS *a platform for the Holy Spirit. The very Spirit of God has chosen to operate through you and in you. He is holy. He loves you so much. He longs to partner with you and live life with you, not just in heaven but here on this earth. He doesn't want the first time you really encounter Him to be in heaven. He wants to flow through you now, flow through you prophetically. The Holy Spirit is here to partner with you, to be your friend, your solace, that place of peace, and your Comforter. The Holy Spirit is also full of power, power to cast out demons, heal the sick, and conquer demonic warfare. Trust Him. Trust Him when you can't see Him or feel Him. Trust Him now, even before you really know Him. Allow Him to move through you. You have a new assignment here on earth, one of accomplishment with Me, with the Holy Spirit. Allow Him access with no restrictions. Allow Him to have His way. Yield to Him. Succumb to Him. Receive revelation from Him and believe you hear from Him. He has a way for you, a way you cannot comprehend. He needs utter reliance and dependence on Him. You need to trust Him with everything that is in you. Your life is His platform. He can reach people through you. You have to trust Him. Trust Him with what you can see and with what you cannot see and understand. Allow Him to consume every part of your being. Connect your spirit with the Holy Spirit. Together you have great things to accomplish. He will bring you to a place of peace and conviction. Embrace the conviction; it brings forth change and acceleration in your spiritual walk. You have a long path to walk out, one I have chartered for you, now do it with the greatest helper that I left you, the Holy Spirit.*

Author's Closing Remarks

You are a platform for the Holy Spirit. He has been my best friend, and I desire for Him to be your best friend. I hope you have grown closer to Him through this book. Live your life for Him. Allow Him to orchestrate and lead every step. Invite Him to ordain your day and to mentor you. I spent two years of my life prostrate on the carpet, having Him teach and instruct me. The only regret I have is all the time I didn't yield to Him or get in His presence. I pray you will have no regrets as you partner with Him.

—Kathy

BIOGRAPHY

KATHY DEGRAW IS a prophetic deliverance minister, releasing the love and power of God to ignite and activate people, release prophetic destinies, and deliver people from the bondage of the enemy. She is the founder of Kathy DeGraw Ministries and K Advancement LLC. She travels internationally, speaking at conferences and bringing her teaching schools around the world.

Kathy hosts a podcast show called *Prophetic Spiritual Warfare*. Kathy is a prophetic voice and writer for the Elijah List, *Charisma* magazine, Prophecy Investigators, and *GODSPEED* magazine. She has published several books, including *Unshackled*, *Discerning and Destroying the Works of Satan*, and *SPEAK OUT*.

She is married to her husband, Pastor Ron. They have three kids: Dillon, Amber (and son-in-law, Josh), and Lauren (and son-in-law, Alex). Her golden retriever puppy dog, Shiloh, is a great companion, sitting by her while she writes.

Be in touch with Kathy at:
kathydegrawministries.org
email: admin@degrawministries.org

Prophetic Spiritual Warfare Podcast
https://www.charismapodcastnetwork.com/
show/propheticspiritualwarfarepodcast

Facebook: Kathy DeGraw
https://www.facebook.com/kathydegraw

Appendix

ADDITIONAL RESOURCES

Podcast

https://www.charismapodcastnetwork.com/show/propheticspiritualwarfarepodcast

E-courses

https://www.charismacourses.com/collections?category=kathy-degraw or www.kathydegrawministries.org

Books

Unshackled: Breaking the Strongholds of Your Past to Receive Complete Deliverance (Bloomington, MN: Chosen Books, 2020)

Discerning and Destroying the Works of Satan: Your Deliverance Guide to Total Freedom (Shippensburg, PA: Destiny Image, 2018)

SPEAK OUT: Releasing the Power of Declaring Prayer (Lake Mary, FL: Creation House, 2017)

Who Is Speaking? Discerning the Source Infiltrating Your Thoughts (n.p.: K Publishing, 2018)

Prophetic Proclamations: Activating the Spirit Realm to Operate in Your Favor (n.p.: K Publishing, 2017)

NOTES

Chapter 4
Spiritual Warfare Is Audible

1. *American Dictionary of the English Language*, s.v. "say," accessed January 26, 2021, http://webstersdictionary1828.com/Dictionary/say.

Chapter 5
Walk in Dominion

1. *English World Dictionary*, s.v. "authority," accessed January 26, 2021, http://world_en.enacademic.com/5576/authority.
2. Blue Letter Bible, s.v. "*radah*," accessed January 27, 2021, https://www.blueletterbible.org/lang/lexicon/lexicon.cfm?Strongs=H7287&t=KJV.

Chapter 6
Build a Warrior's Heart

1. *American Dictionary of the English Language*, s.v. "reverence," accessed January 27, 2021, http://webstersdictionary1828.com/Dictionary/reverence.
2. *Merriam-Webster*, s.v. "veneration," accessed January 27, 2021, https://www.merriam-webster.com/dictionary/veneration.
3. *Merriam-Webster*, s.v. "filial," accessed January 27, 2021, https://www.merriam-webster.com/dictionary/filial.
4. "KJV Dictionary Definition: Revere," AV1611, accessed January 27, 2021, https://av1611.com/kjbp/kjv-dictionary/revere.html.
5. "The Power of 'I Love You' From Dad," National Center for Fathering, accessed January 27, 2021, https://fathers.com/featured-resource-center-page/the-power-of-i-love-you-from-dad/.
6. Blue Letter Bible, s.v. "*yashab*," accessed January 27, 2021, https://www.blueletterbible.org/lang/lexicon/lexicon.cfm?Strongs=H3427&t=KJV.

7. Blue Letter Bible, s.v. "*luwn*," accessed January 27, 2021, https://www.blueletterbible.org/lang/lexicon/lexicon.cfm?Strongs=H3885&t=KJV.

Chapter 9

Conquer Every Thought

1. Kathy DeGraw, "How to Guard Your Thoughts From the Enemy," *Charisma*, February 10, 2016, https://www.charismamag.com/spirit/spiritual-warfare/25548-how-to-guard-your-thoughts.

Chapter 10

Rebuke and Expose Demonic Assignments

1. *Merriam-Webster*, s.v. "ransack," accessed January 28, 2021, https://www.merriam-webster.com/dictionary/ransack.
2. *American Dictionary of the English Language*, s.v. "sentinel," accessed January 28, 2021, http://webstersdictionary1828.com/Dictionary/sentinel.
3. Blue Letter Bible, s.v. "*pythōn*," accessed January 28, 2021, https://www.blueletterbible.org/lang/lexicon/lexicon.cfm?Strongs=G4436&t=KJV.

Chapter 13

Breaking Agreement

1. *American Dictionary of the English Language*, s.v. "renounce," accessed January 29, 2021, http://webstersdictionary1828.com/Dictionary/renounce.